KING
HUSSEIN

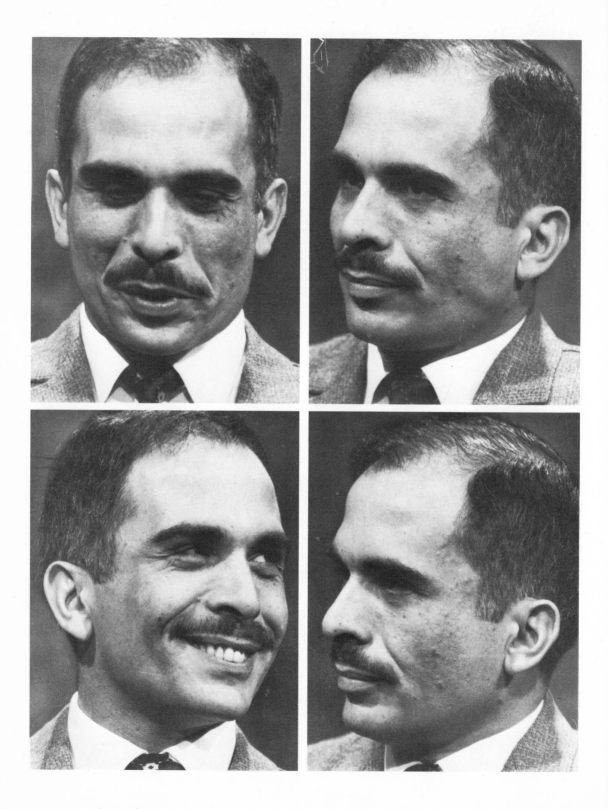

KING HUSSEIN

Gregory Matusky
and
John P. Hayes

CHELSEA HOUSE PUBLISHERS
NEW YORK
NEW HAVEN   PHILADELPHIA

MC 206 1291√

EDITORIAL DIRECTOR: Nancy Toff
MANAGING EDITOR: Karyn Gullen Browne
COPY CHIEF: Perry Scott King
ART DIRECTOR: Giannella Garrett
ASSISTANT ART DIRECTOR: Carol McDougall
PICTURE EDITOR: Elizabeth Terhune

Staff for KING HUSSEIN

SENIOR EDITOR: John W. Selfridge
ASSISTANT EDITORS: Maria Behan, Pierre Hauser, Howard Ratner, Bert Yaeger
COPY EDITORS: Sean Dolan, Kathleen McDermott
ASSISTANT DESIGNER: Noreen Lamb
PICTURE RESEARCH: Juliette Dickstein
LAYOUT: Irene Friedman
PRODUCTION COORDINATOR: Alma Rodriguez
PRODUCTION ASSISTANT: Karen Dreste
COVER ILLUSTRATION: Richard Leonard

CREATIVE DIRECTOR: Harold Steinberg

Frontispiece courtesy of AP/Wide World

3 5 7 9 8 6 4 2

Library of Congress Cataloging in Publication Data

Hayes, John Phillip. KING HUSSEIN

(World leaders past & present)
Bibliography: p.
Includes index.
1. Hussein, King of Jordan, 1935–   —Juvenile
literature. 2. Jordan—Kings and rulers—Biography—
Juvenile literature. [1. Hussein, King of Jordan, 1935–
2. Kings, queens, rulers, etc.] I. Matusky, Gregory. II. Title.
III. Series.
DS154.55.H8H39   1987   956.95'04'0924 [B] [92]   86-24486

ISBN 0-87754-533-2

Contents

"On Leadership," Arthur M. Schlesinger, jr. 7
1. Life in a Desert Kingdom 13
2. Bloodshed Begins. 27
3. From Schoolboy to King 39
4. Hussein and Nasser 49
5. Threats from All Sides 61
6. Prosperity Gives Way to Defeat 73
7. A Country Divided. 85
8. The Road to Peace 97
Further Reading. 108
Chronology. 109
Index. 110

John Adams
John Quincy Adams
Konrad Adenauer
Alexander the Great
Salvador Allende
Marc Antony
Corazon Aquino
Yasir Arafat
King Arthur
Hafez al-Assad
Kemal Atatürk
Attila
Clement Attlee
Augustus Caesar
Menachem Begin
David Ben-Gurion
Otto von Bismarck
Léon Blum
Simon Bolívar
Cesare Borgia
Willy Brandt
Leonid Brezhnev
Julius Caesar
John Calvin
Jimmy Carter
Fidel Castro
Catherine the Great
Charlemagne
Chiang Kai-Shek
Winston Churchill
Georges Clemenceau
Cleopatra
Constantine the Great
Hernán Cortés
Oliver Cromwell
Georges-Jacques
  Danton
Jefferson Davis
Moshe Dayan
Charles de Gaulle
Eamon De Valera
Eugene Debs
Deng Xiaoping
Benjamin Disraeli
Alexander Dubček
François & Jean-Claude
  Duvalier
Dwight Eisenhower
Eleanor of Aquitaine
Elizabeth I
Faisal
Ferdinand & Isabella
Francisco Franco
Benjamin Franklin

Frederick the Great
Indira Gandhi
Mohandas Gandhi
Giuseppe Garibaldi
Amin & Bashir Gemayel
Genghis Khan
William Gladstone
Mikhail Gorbachev
Ulysses S. Grant
Ernesto "Che" Guevara
Tenzin Gyatso
Alexander Hamilton
Dag Hammarskjöld
Henry VIII
Henry of Navarre
Paul von Hindenburg
Hirohito
Adolf Hitler
Ho Chi Minh
King Hussein
Ivan the Terrible
Andrew Jackson
James I
Wojciech Jaruzelski
Thomas Jefferson
Joan of Arc
Pope John XXIII
Pope John Paul II
Lyndon Johnson
Benito Juárez
John Kennedy
Robert Kennedy
Jomo Kenyatta
Ayatollah Khomeini
Nikita Khrushchev
Kim Il Sung
Martin Luther King, Jr.
Henry Kissinger
Kublai Khan
Lafayette
Robert E. Lee
Vladimir Lenin
Abraham Lincoln
David Lloyd George
Louis XIV
Martin Luther
Judas Maccabeus
James Madison
Nelson & Winnie
  Mandela
Mao Zedong
Ferdinand Marcos
George Marshall

Mary, Queen of Scots
Tomáš Masaryk
Golda Meir
Klemens von Metternich
James Monroe
Hosni Mubarak
Robert Mugabe
Benito Mussolini
Napoléon Bonaparte
Gamal Abdel Nasser
Jawaharlal Nehru
Nero
Nicholas II
Richard Nixon
Kwame Nkrumah
Daniel Ortega
Mohammed Reza Pahlavi
Thomas Paine
Charles Stewart
  Parnell
Pericles
Juan Perón
Peter the Great
Pol Pot
Muammar el-Qaddafi
Ronald Reagan
Cardinal Richelieu
Maximilien Robespierre
Eleanor Roosevelt
Franklin Roosevelt
Theodore Roosevelt
Anwar Sadat
Haile Selassie
Prince Sihanouk
Jan Smuts
Joseph Stalin
Sukarno
Sun Yat-sen
Tamerlane
Mother Teresa
Margaret Thatcher
Josip Broz Tito
Toussaint L'Ouverture
Leon Trotsky
Pierre Trudeau
Harry Truman
Queen Victoria
Lech Walesa
George Washington
Chaim Weizmann
Woodrow Wilson
Xerxes
Emiliano Zapata
Zhou Enlai

CHELSEA HOUSE PUBLISHERS

ON LEADERSHIP

Arthur M. Schlesinger, jr.

LEADERSHIP, it may be said, is really what makes the world go round. Love no doubt smooths the passage; but love is a private transaction between consenting adults. Leadership is a public transaction with history. The idea of leadership affirms the capacity of individuals to move, inspire, and mobilize masses of people so that they act together in pursuit of an end. Sometimes leadership serves good purposes, sometimes bad; but whether the end is benign or evil, great leaders are those men and women who leave their personal stamp on history.

Now, the very concept of leadership implies the proposition that individuals can make a difference. This proposition has never been universally accepted. From classical times to the present day, eminent thinkers have regarded individuals as no more than the agents and pawns of larger forces, whether the gods and goddesses of the ancient world or, in the modern era, race, class, nation, the dialectic, the will of the people, the spirit of the times, history itself. Against such forces, the individual dwindles into insignificance.

So contends the thesis of historical determinism. Tolstoy's great novel *War and Peace* offers a famous statement of the case. Why, Tolstoy asked, did millions of men in the Napoleonic Wars, denying their human feelings and their common sense, move back and forth across Europe slaughtering their fellows? "The war," Tolstoy answered, "was bound to happen simply because it was bound to happen." All prior history predetermined it. As for leaders, they, Tolstoy said, "are but the labels that serve to give a name to an end and, like labels, they have the least possible connection with the event." The greater the leader, "the more conspicuous the inevitability and the predestination of every act he commits." The leader, said Tolstoy, is "the slave of history."

Determinism takes many forms. Marxism is the determinism of class. Nazism the determinism of race. But the idea of men and women as the slaves of history runs athwart the deepest human instincts. Rigid determinism abolishes the idea of human freedom—

the assumption of free choice that underlies every move we make, every word we speak, every thought we think. It abolishes the idea of human responsibility, since it is manifestly unfair to reward or punish people for actions that are by definition beyond their control. No one can live consistently by any deterministic creed. The Marxist states prove this themselves by their extreme susceptibility to the cult of leadership.

More than that, history refutes the idea that individuals make no difference. In December 1931 a British politician crossing Park Avenue in New York City between 76th and 77th Streets around 10:30 P.M. looked in the wrong direction and was knocked down by an automobile—a moment, he later recalled, of a man aghast, a world aglare: "I do not understand why I was not broken like an eggshell or squashed like a gooseberry." Fourteen months later an American politician, sitting in an open car in Miami, Florida, was fired on by an assassin; the man beside him was hit. Those who believe that individuals make no difference to history might well ponder whether the next two decades would have been the same had Mario Constasino's car killed Winston Churchill in 1931 and Giuseppe Zangara's bullet killed Franklin Roosevelt in 1933. Suppose, in addition, that Adolf Hitler had been killed in the street fighting during the Munich *Putsch* of 1923 and that Lenin had died of typhus during World War I. What would the 20th century be like now?

For better or for worse, individuals do make a difference. "The notion that a people can run itself and its affairs anonymously," wrote the philosopher William James, "is now well known to be the silliest of absurdities. Mankind does nothing save through initiatives on the part of inventors, great or small, and imitation by the rest of us—these are the sole factors in human progress. Individuals of genius show the way, and set the patterns, which common people then adopt and follow."

Leadership, James suggests, means leadership in thought as well as in action. In the long run, leaders in thought may well make the greater difference to the world. But, as Woodrow Wilson once said, "Those only are leaders of men, in the general eye, who lead in action. . . . It is at their hands that new thought gets its translation into the crude language of deeds." Leaders in thought often invent in solitude and obscurity, leaving to later generations the tasks of imitation. Leaders in action—the leaders portrayed in this series—have to be effective in their own time.

And they cannot be effective by themselves. They must act in response to the rhythms of their age. Their genius must be adapted, in a phrase of William James's, "to the receptivities of the moment." Leaders are useless without followers. "There goes the mob," said the French politician hearing a clamor in the streets. "I am their leader. I must follow them." Great leaders turn the inchoate emotions of the mob to purposes of their own. They seize on the opportunities of their time, the hopes, fears, frustrations, crises, potentialities. They succeed when events have prepared the way for them, when the community is awaiting to be aroused, when they can provide the clarifying and organizing ideas. Leadership ignites the circuit between the individual and the mass and thereby alters history.

It may alter history for better or for worse. Leaders have been responsible for the most extravagant follies and most monstrous crimes that have beset suffering humanity. They have also been vital in such gains as humanity has made in individual freedom, religious and racial tolerance, social justice, and respect for human rights.

There is no sure way to tell in advance who is going to lead for good and who for evil. But a glance at the gallery of men and women in *World Leaders—Past and Present* suggests some useful tests.

One test is this: Do leaders lead by force or by persuasion? By command or by consent? Through most of history leadership was exercised by the divine right of authority. The duty of followers was to defer and to obey. "Theirs not to reason why / Theirs but to do and die." On occasion, as with the so-called enlightened despots of the 18th century in Europe, absolutist leadership was animated by humane purposes. More often, absolutism nourished the passion for domination, land, gold, and conquest and resulted in tyranny.

The great revolution of modern times has been the revolution of equality. The idea that all people should be equal in their legal condition has undermined the old structure of authority, hierarchy, and deference. The revolution of equality has had two contrary effects on the nature of leadership. For equality, as Alexis de Tocqueville pointed out in his great study *Democracy in America,* might mean equality in servitude as well as equality in freedom.

"I know of only two methods of establishing equality in the political world," Tocqueville wrote. "Rights must be given to every citizen, or none at all to anyone . . . save one, who is the master of all." There was no middle ground "between the sovereignty of all and the absolute power of one man." In his astonishing prediction of 20th-century totalitarian dictatorship, Tocqueville explained how the revolution of equality could lead to the *"Führerprinzip"* and more terrible absolutism than the world had ever known.

But when rights are given to every citizen and the sovereignty of all is established, the problem of leadership takes a new form, becomes more exacting than ever before. It is easy to issue commands and enforce them by the rope and the stake, the concentration camp and the *gulag.* It is much harder to use argument and achievement to overcome opposition and win consent. The Founding Fathers of the United States understood the difficulty. They believed that history had given them the opportunity to decide, as Alexander Hamilton wrote in the first Federalist Paper, whether men are indeed capable of basing government on "reflection and choice, or whether they are forever destined to depend . . . on accident and force."

Government by reflection and choice called for a new style of leadership and a new quality of followership. It required leaders to be responsive to popular concerns, and it required followers to be active and informed participants in the process. Democracy does not eliminate emotion from politics; sometimes it fosters demagoguery; but it is confident that, as the greatest of democratic leaders put it, you cannot fool all of the people all of the time. It measures leadership by results and retires those who overreach or falter or fail.

It is true that in the long run despots are measured by results too. But they can postpone the day of judgment, sometimes indefinitely, and in the meantime they can do infinite harm. It is also true that democracy is no guarantee of virtue and intelligence in government, for the voice of the people is not necessarily the voice of God. But democracy, by assuring the right of opposition, offers built-in resistance to the evils inherent in absolutism. As the theologian Reinhold Niebuhr summed it up, "Man's capacity for justice makes democracy possible, but man's inclination to injustice makes democracy necessary."

A second test for leadership is the end for which power is sought. When leaders have as their goal the supremacy of a master race or the promotion of totalitarian revolution or the acquisition and exploitation of colonies or the protection of greed and privilege or the preservation of personal power, it is likely that their leadership will do little to advance the cause of humanity. When their goal is the abolition of slavery, the liberation of women, the enlargement of opportunity for the poor and powerless, the extension of equal rights to racial minorities, the defense of the freedoms of expression and opposition, it is likely that their leadership will increase the sum of human liberty and welfare.

Leaders have done great harm to the world. They have also conferred great benefits. You will find both sorts in this series. Even "good" leaders must be regarded with a certain wariness. Leaders are not demigods; they put on their trousers one leg after another just like ordinary mortals. No leader is infallible, and every leader needs to be reminded of this at regular intervals. Irreverence irritates leaders but is their salvation. Unquestioning submission corrupts leaders and demeans followers. Making a cult of a leader is always a mistake. Fortunately hero worship generates its own antidote. "Every hero," said Emerson, "becomes a bore at last."

The signal benefit the great leaders confer is to embolden the rest of us to live according to our own best selves, to be active, insistent, and resolute in affirming our own sense of things. For great leaders attest to the reality of human freedom against the supposed inevitabilities of history. And they attest to the wisdom and power that may lie within the most unlikely of us, which is why Abraham Lincoln remains the supreme example of great leadership. A great leader, said Emerson, exhibits new possibilities to all humanity. "We feed on genius. . . . Great men exist that there may be greater men."

Great leaders, in short, justify themselves by emancipating and empowering their followers. So humanity struggles to master its destiny, remembering with Alexis de Tocqueville: "It is true that around every man a fatal circle is traced beyond which he cannot pass; but within the wide verge of that circle he is powerful and free; as it is with man, so with communities."

1

Life in a Desert Kingdom

Hussein ibn Talal, king of Jordan, stood alone on a hill and surveyed the destruction that lay before him. A once strong army was now a mass of rubble and wreckage. The king's forces had been destroyed in three days by a smaller but more cunning enemy. Hussein watched solemnly as plumes of thick, oily smoke rose from the twisted, smoldering armor, his nose filled with the smell of burning paint and metal. He heard the sound of distant bombs and flinched when enemy jet fighters thundered overhead. Hussein saw the sprawled bodies of brave Jordanian soldiers baking in the hot June sun.

The Six-Day War of 1967 had ended. The allied Arab forces of Egypt, Jordan, Syria, and Iraq had lost to Israel. Jordan's involvement had lasted only three days, yet 6,000 of the king's men had died in the fighting. Most of his army had been ruined. Jordanian equipment and many weapons had fallen into enemy hands. The king's military showpiece, his air force, had been annihilated.

Far worse was the kingdom's loss of land. Jordan had surrendered its part of the historic city of Jerusalem in the war and had lost its claim to such age-old cities as Bethlehem and Jericho. The rich West Bank area along the Jordan River had also fallen to Israel. Israeli forces now roamed freely over territory that was once Jordan's and stood only 15

> *The end of the Israeli war had left the whole Arab world stunned, angry and discontented. Even at sixteen I could feel the atmosphere growing, slowly enveloping the countryside like a cloud of poison gas.*
> —HUSSEIN
> on Arab discontent in 1951

Hussein ibn Talal, king of Jordan, salutes his troops in August 1969. The years following the 1967 Six-Day War were particularly hard for Jordan. After the country's devastating defeat by Israel, Hussein faced the formidable task of not only rebuilding his military, but also of rethinking Jordan's role in the Middle East.

miles from Amman, Jordan's capital city. Jordan had seen better times.

Jordan, or Transjordan, as it was known before 1946, was then, as it is now, a small country with a land area no bigger than South Carolina. It is located in the Middle East, northeast of Africa and south of Eastern Europe. To the north are Lebanon and Syria. Iraq lies to the east and Saudi Arabia to the south. Israel (before 1948 known as Palestine) sits on Jordan's western border.

In Hussein's own words: "Jordan itself is a beautiful country. It is wild, with limitless deserts . . . but the mountains of the north are clothed in green forests, and where the Jordan River flows it is fertile and warm in winter. Jordan has a strange, haunting beauty and a sense of timelessness. Dotted with the ruins of empires once great, it is the last resort of yesterday and tomorrow."

In fact, the ancient Romans once used Jordan as a place to trade goods with merchants from the Far East and Africa. The stone walls and arches of Roman theaters and aqueducts still dot the countryside. With the decline of the Eastern Roman Empire in the 7th century A.D., the land fell under the control of Arab conquerors from the south. The Arabs brought with them their religion, Islam, which had arisen near the city of Mecca (now in Saudi Arabia). Islam became dominant in the Jordanian region, and its followers were known as Muslims.

In the southern and eastern parts of Jordan, where rocky hills give way to rolling sand dunes, seemingly endless deserts spread over lands inhabited by Bedouins. Fiercely independent, Bedouins are a proud people known for their lively spirit and strong devotion to the Islamic religion. Upon their camels, Bedouins roam over great expanses of desert in search of water and grass for their grazing sheep. They never have had permanent homes and for the most part continue to live in small groups far from towns and cities.

This was the exotic desert country into which Hussein was born on November 14, 1935. He was the oldest of four children and the son of Crown

Prince Talal and Queen Zain. Yet it was his grandfather, King Abdullah, ruler of Jordan, who was the strongest influence in young Hussein's life.

Abdullah was a strong-willed, domineering man, who led more by his personality than by reason. He embraced friends warmly but opposed his enemies ruthlessly and sometimes violently. During his reign, Abdullah defeated many attempted revolts through the might of his army. Later in his life, he became so paranoid about these revolts that his bodyguards had to fasten his sword to its scabbard to keep him from raising it against innocent people.

Abdullah was also easy to like. He loved life and enjoyed its many pleasures. T. E. Lawrence, better known as "Lawrence of Arabia," an Englishman who fought alongside the Arabs against the Turks in World War I, did not believe Abdullah had a serious enough nature to be a great ruler. "Before

Israeli soldiers at the dedication of a settlement on the Israeli-occupied West Bank of the Jordan River. Since Israel seized the 2,270 square miles of land from Jordan in the 1967 war, the West Bank has been a region over which the two nations have been in hot dispute.

long, I began to suspect him of constant cheerfulness. His eyes had a confirmed twinkle," Lawrence wrote. Abdullah was famous for having installed a set of distorting mirrors in the entrance to his palace and then chuckling at the changing shapes of approaching diplomats.

Yet the king held great power in his desert kingdom. Abdullah was of Bedouin ancestry, and the Bedouin population of Jordan supported him firmly. Throughout his life, he retained many of his desert traditions. Hussein later explained that the Bedouin life "is based on three virtues — honor, courage, and hospitality. We believe that to be an honorable man you must have the courage to defend your honor. We believe that you must always show hospitality. What is yours belongs also to your guests. Even an enemy has the guarantee of shelter and food once he reaches the camp of any tribe." Bedouins still talk of the time the king tracked down

Jordan, a crescent of mostly desert land, has the longest border with Israel of any of the Arab countries. Surrounded on three sides by the much bigger states of Syria, Iraq, and Saudi Arabia, Jordan also has had to maintain a delicate balance in its relationship with its Arab neighbors.

AP/WIDE WORLD PHOTOS

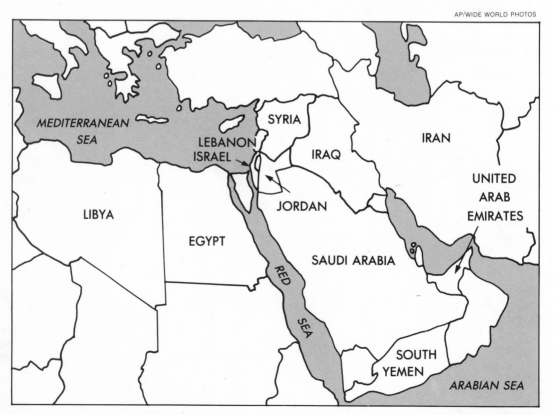

16

a scoundrel who made a poor woman pregnant. On cool evenings, Abdullah received subjects while relaxing in desert tents erected on palace grounds. Even the poorest person could plead his case before the king.

Abdullah was born in the early 1880s near the holy city of Mecca in the desert region of Hejaz. The great Islamic prophet, Muhammad, had been born in Mecca in 570 A.D. Abdullah and his family belonged to the Hashemite dynasty, which claimed descent from Muhammad and for centuries had guarded Mecca from enemies of Islam. Abdullah's family enjoyed great power and respect because of their relationship to the Prophet.

The family's influence was so great that when the Ottoman Turks captured the Hejaz area in the 16th century they required that a member of the Hashemite family should always be held as a hostage to keep the region's people from rebelling. Abdullah's father, Hussein ibn Ali, spent 15 years as a hostage to this Turkish empire, which ruled great parts of northern Africa, Asia, southern Europe, and Arabia. He was finally released in 1908 on the death of his uncle, the *emir*, or leader, of Mecca, so that he might claim the vacant office and swear allegiance to the empire.

Once at Mecca, Hussein ibn Ali denounced the Turkish oppressors, leading to a much less stable relationship with the empire. When World War I broke out in 1914, the Hashemites saw an opportunity to reestablish their power.

Hussein ibn Ali's second son, Abdullah, traveled to Cairo, Egypt, to meet with Lord Horatio Kitchener, the British military commander. Britain was fighting the Germans in Europe at the time and had great economic and strategic interests in the Middle East. The Hashemites were looking for allies against the Turks. Abdullah told Kitchener that the Hashemites would no longer accept Turkish rule and would fight alongside Britain if war broke out in the Middle East.

When the Ottoman Empire entered the war in November 1914 on the side of Germany, British-backed Hashemite forces revolted against the

But give glad tidings to those who believe and work righteousness, that their portion is the Gardens, beneath which rivers flow.
—from the Koran

Turks. In return for their efforts, the British promised the Hashemites their own Arab state, including what is now Jordan, Syria, Israel, Lebanon, the Arabian peninsula, and northern regions of Iraq. The Hashemites fought courageously. They recaptured much of the land occupied by the empire. Abdullah's younger brother, Faisal, defeated the Turks at Aqaba, an important port on a gulf connected to the Red Sea. He then advanced north through what is now Jordan and freed Syria from Ottoman rule. Abdullah stayed close to home and overpowered the Turkish forces defending the Muslim holy cities of Mecca and Medina. On November 2, 1916, Hussein ibn Ali assumed the title of king of the Hejaz.

After the fall of the Ottoman Empire in 1918, the Hashemites expected the land to formally come under their rule, but they were double-crossed when Britain secretly struck the Sykes-Picot Agreement with France. Under this pact the two countries divided the Middle East between themselves, disregarding all claims of the Hashemites, who were left with only the Arabian peninsula. The French expelled Faisal from Syria in 1920 and took control of Lebanon. Britain claimed Palestine (Israel) and the northern provinces of Iraq. The Transjordan region also fell under British mandate (administrative authority).

Abdullah, however, was undaunted by the dishonest dealings of the Europeans. In late 1920 he gathered his supporters and boarded a train on the rickety Turkish railroad to Jordan. There, in the extreme heat of the desert, he staked a claim to the land east of Palestine. At first, neither the British nor the Bedouins took him seriously, since he had no army or wealth. But Abdullah relied on his holy name and self-assured style to establish authority in this bit of desert.

The British quietly recognized Abdullah's rule. Winston Churchill, then colonial secretary for Britain, met Abdullah in Jerusalem in 1922 and offered him financial and military support. The British wanted to establish a political presence in the Middle East and believed that by helping Abdullah their objective would be met. They sweetened the offer by

An Arab sidewalk cafe in Jerusalem, the ancient city holy to Jews, Muslims, and Christians. The eastern part of the city — called the Old City — in which are located monuments sacred to all three religions, belonged to Jordan until its capture and annexation by Israel in 1967.

The Jordan River, part of the boundary between Israel and Jordan, winds its way through the desert. On the western side of the river lies the area of Judea, containing the ancient cities of Jerusalem, Bethlehem, and Jericho, which belonged to Jordan from 1948 to 1967.

A Bedouin girl in Petra, Jordan. The Bedouins have traditionally been an independent, nomadic people, roaming the deserts of the southern and eastern parts of Jordan with their herds of camels, sheep, and goats. Almost all of Jordan's population was Bedouin when the kingdom was created in the early 1920s.

including something for Abdullah's brother, Faisal, in the deal. He would be given the kingdom of Iraq to make amends for losing Syria. First, however, Abdullah had to accept a British mandate over the region. The British also made it clear that they would stand by their 1917 Balfour Declaration. This proclamation stated that Jewish people from around the world would be given their own homeland, in a region of Palestine west of the Jordan River. This area later became Israel.

Abdullah agreed to the terms and established his government. It was a monarchy — that is, the king held absolute power over the land and its people. In 1939 the Jordanian Parliament was created as a check on the absolute power of the king. Jordan's government became a constitutional monarchy. Even after the British mandate was abolished and Jordan declared its independence in May 1946, Britain was bound to a relationship that would continue through many troubled years. It was a partner in a region that to this day is burdened by violence and bloodshed. The Hashemite dynasty gained lands that spread in a crescent from the Persian Gulf to the tip of Egypt.

Hussein's grandfather, Abdullah, had single-handedly carved out a country for himself. Though the Hashemites were now considered the royal family of Jordan, they enjoyed few special rights or privileges, for Jordan was a poor country and could not afford extravagance. Hussein's family lived a simple

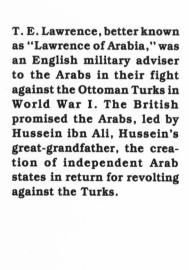

T. E. Lawrence, better known as "Lawrence of Arabia," was an English military adviser to the Arabs in their fight against the Ottoman Turks in World War I. The British promised the Arabs, led by Hussein ibn Ali, Hussein's great-grandfather, the creation of independent Arab states in return for revolting against the Turks.

King Abdullah, ruler of Jordan from 1920 to 1951, holds a conference in the courtyard of his palace at Amman in 1948. Abdullah, grandfather of King Hussein, was a Hashemite, a member of a powerful Arab family that claims to be directly descended from Muhammad, the founder of Islam.

The royal palace in Amman. After the collapse of the Ottoman Empire in 1918, Britain and France divided the Middle East between themselves. Unconcerned with foreign arrangements, Abdullah laid his own claim in 1920 to the lands east of the Jordan River, founding the modern state of Jordan.

life on a hill overlooking their capital of Amman. Their home was a modest, gray stone structure with five large rooms that let in cool breezes to blow away the desert heat.

The family's only money came from a small allowance given to them by the government. In his autobiography, Hussein wrote of a bicycle his cousin Faisal once gave him. It was red with shiny chrome fenders. Hussein took loving care of the gift until his mother was forced to sell it to pay a family debt. The queen consoled her son by asking him to be brave. "You know that all through life you will have to stand up to disappointments," she said. "Be brave; one day you will forget this bicycle when you are older and are driving big, shiny cars." Indeed, Hussein later drove fast and powerful cars, but he credits his humble beginnings with teaching him the true value of money.

Much of Hussein's early life was spent on that hill above Amman. He attended nursery and elementary school there. His friends and teachers remember him as a quiet child who received below-average grades. He knew many of his classmates but felt close to few.

As he grew older, Hussein joined his father, Talal, on hunting trips. They would travel to oases in the desert and shoot ducks or gazelle. Theirs was a close relationship, and Hussein loved his father and respected his gentle kindness.

Talal had little interest in politics. Instead, he enjoyed the simple pleasures of family and friends. Hussein often talks of his father's great charm. "I never met a man who did not like him. His honesty was known throughout the kingdom," he says. Hussein fondly recalls the hours spent listening to his father tell stories of times long past. Talal's love united Hussein's family.

King Abdullah, however, now dreamed of passing his power on to his sons. But neither man was suited to be king. Abdullah's son Naif was only half Hashemite, and therefore considered unacceptable. His other son, Talal, seemed a logical choice. He was intelligent and well liked. But Talal suffered from schizophrenia, a severe mental disorder that affects thinking processes. At first Talal's periods of madness were controllable and merely embarrassing to the royal family. But as he grew older the condition became worse. Talal flew into violent rages and attacked people around him. He disappeared for hours, only to be found later wandering aimlessly in the desert. The palace guards locked the royal stables so he could not ride off in an angry fit.

Abdullah was insensitive to Talal's suffering. He could not sympathize with his son's condition, and he considered the illness a weakness of character. "He had wanted a brave, intrepid Bedouin son to carry on the great Arab revolt. He was incapable of accepting an invalid in place of his dream," Hussein wrote. "It was the bitterest disappointment of his life." So Abdullah turned his love to Hussein.

Many men were afraid of him, but not I. He loved me very much, that I know, and I in my turn loved him to the point where I no longer feared his rather austere outward appearance, and I think he knew and appreciated this. To me he was more than a grandfather, and to him I think I was a son.
—HUSSEIN
on his grandfather,
King Abdullah

2

Bloodshed Begins

On a cool summer evening in July 1951, Hussein and his 69-year-old grandfather sat in a Bedouin tent and discussed the day's events, as well as plans for their upcoming trip to Jerusalem. It was a common sight. On many evenings, the two sat together on silk pillows and talked. Yet that night's conversation was different. Gone was King Abdullah's usual energy and animation. Instead, a calm and thoughtful mood prevailed. He turned to his grandson and in a gentle voice said, "I hope you realize, my son, that one day you will have to assume responsibility. I look to you to do your very best to see that my work is not lost. I look to you to continue it in the service of our people." Fifteen-year-old Hussein looked deeply into his grandfather's eyes and solemnly promised to do as he was asked.

Hussein was then a boarding-school student living and studying at Victoria College in Alexandria, Egypt. It was a happy period in Hussein's life. Victoria College was an exclusive preparatory school modeled after British secondary schools. King Abdullah paid the expensive tuition. Hussein felt comfortable among the many students who came from other Middle Eastern countries. At Victoria Hussein was not treated like royalty, he was simply a student like all the other boys. He received no special privileges and did his own chores. "I can remember sitting one afternoon on the edge of my bed, after I

> *When I have to die, I would like to be shot in the head by a nobody. That's the simplest way of dying. I would rather have that than become old and a burden.*
> —ABDULLAH
> hours before his assassination on July 20, 1951

Hussein in 1952, at the age of 17, in royal dress. Due to his father Talal's mental instability, and his uncle Naif's lack of full Hashemite ancestry, Hussein was King Abdullah's chosen successor for the throne of Jordan.

had torn my blazer, struggling to thread a borrowed needle and finally sewing up the tear," Hussein later wrote.

He studied Arabic and religion, and earned good grades. He also became a skilled fencer and received a medal in the sport during his last term. King Abdullah was so pleased that he made his grandson an honorary captain in the Jordanian army and issued him a uniform with silver medals.

But all was not well in Jordan. During the 1940s King Abdullah was severely criticized for his close friendship with Britain. In the late 1940s Abdullah allowed British troops to roam freely over Jordanian territory. John Bagot Glubb, a British military officer, led the Jordanian army. British money bought guns, trained recruits, and fed the Bedouin soldiers. Funds from Britain also supported the country's economy. With little agriculture and no industry, Jordan's only source of income came from the British government in faraway London.

Abdullah's dependence on Britain placed him at odds with other Arab countries. Many Arab people dreamed of one Arab nation free from outside influence and united by Islamic law. The movement was known as Arab nationalism. Abdullah's close relationship with Britain conflicted with Arab nationalism because it undermined Jordan's status as an independent country.

Also unsettling to the region was the establishment of Israel, the Jewish nation founded after World War II. The Jewish people had struggled for many years to create a homeland in Palestine. Before World War II, Palestine's population was mostly Arab. In 1947, however, the United Nations acknowledged Jewish claims to the area and divided the land into two sections — one Jewish and the other Arab — under temporary British supervision. Neither state was independent but each was promised independence at a later date.

Arabs in Palestine and other parts of the Middle East were outraged by the partition. They refused to accept Jewish authority over lands that Arabs once controlled. They swore to avenge their loss.

On May 14, 1948, Israel boldly declared itself in-

dependent. Infuriated by the declaration, armies from five Arab countries attacked the new nation the very next day.

The war lasted nine months. Arab forces were disorganized and poorly prepared. Israel won easily. Thousands of Arab Palestinians living in what is now Israel lost their homes. They were refugees, people without a country.

Jordan's army, led by General John Glubb, had won a small part of Palestine in the West Bank region on the Jordan River. The victory was a mixed blessing, however. Nearly a half million Palestinians living on the West Bank became Jordanian citizens. Another quarter million Palestinians, whose lands

Bedouins sit in a tent, their rugs and blankets piled behind them. Many of the nomads entered the army and became some of King Abdullah's most loyal subjects. Abdullah, who was of Bedouin descent, maintained traditional Arab ways and often set up Bedouin tents in the royal courtyard.

29

King Abdullah sits with staff officers of the Iraqi army in 1948. At this time, the Jordanian army was led primarily by British officers. Many Arabs felt that Jordan's continuing dependence on British aid undermined the country's ability to set its own foreign policy.

were occupied by the Israelis, migrated to the small, poor country of Jordan after the war. Jordan was forever changed. Palestinians outnumbered Jordanians two to one within the country. Jordan became home to two separate peoples, each with very different goals and values.

The Palestinians were ambitious and intelligent people. Many had been merchants before the war and held little loyalty to Jordan or its king. On the other hand, Jordan's Bedouins were extremely devoted to their king's holy name and did not want further bloodshed.

Abdullah gave the Palestinian refugees only a small role in the government. The Palestinians, who now dominated the population, resented the token gesture and quickly began planning their return to Palestine.

Through all the turmoil, Abdullah and his grandson, Hussein, grew closer. When home from school, Hussein spent long hours with his grandfather. In the morning they shared light breakfasts of dark Bedouin coffee, bread, butter, and jam. During the day, Hussein worked as a translator for Abdullah, who could understand but not speak English. Hussein would accompany his grandfather to meetings and interpret the words of diplomats from around the world. Late at night, as the king played chess, Hussein listened to Abdullah talk about the hazards of being king. The boy remained by Abdullah's side until dismissed.

The two shared many special moments, including Hussein's early experience driving a car. When he was only 15 years old, Hussein learned to drive, against his parents' wishes. One evening, after dining with Abdullah, the young boy bid his grandfather good-bye and quietly left the palace. As he prepared to drive away, Abdullah appeared in front of the automobile to wish him luck.

"I see you are going home," the king said.

"Yes, sir," Hussein stammered, embarrassed that his grandfather had caught him in the car.

"Well, take it easy — be careful," was all Abdullah said to the boy.

When Hussein returned home, the telephone rang. It was Abdullah making sure young Hussein had arrived safely. The king never told Hussein's parents about the incident.

Hussein once wrote about all that he had learned from Abdullah: "It was he who taught me to understand the minds of my people and the intricacies of the Arab world in which we lived. He taught me the courtly functions, how to behave, and — perhaps because he was a sadly disappointed man who had been deceived by the British and French — how to come to terms with adversity as well as with success. And he taught me above all else that a leader's greatest duty is to serve." Hussein learned well. Then a gunshot cut short the lessons.

The gun was fired on a summer's day in 1951 while Abdullah and Hussein were in Jerusalem to pray at a mosque, an Islamic house of worship. Hussein was excited about accompanying Abdullah to pray in Jerusalem. The young man originally was not scheduled to join Abdullah at the mosque, but the king had a difficult time finding traveling companions that week. "You know, my son, I have asked many people to come with me to Jerusalem tomor-

He was a man of desert ways who had been brought up as a child among the Bedouin tribes. He was fierce and warlike and woe betide the enemy who crossed him. He always felt, to his dying day, that he had been a leading figure in the struggle for Arab independence.
—HUSSEIN
on his grandfather,
King Abdullah

31

row," Abdullah told Hussein before leaving. "It is strange; some of them don't want to come. They seem worried about something happening. I have never heard so many feeble excuses in all my life!"

There were reasons for the excuses. The Arab world was still a troubled place. Traveling among the Arab people was risky. Abdullah received repeated warnings not to journey to Jerusalem. The United States ambassador met with the king before his departure and urged him not to go. "I have heard there may be an attempt on your life. I beseech you, sir, to change your plans," the ambassador pleaded. Abdullah looked at him thoughtfully. "I thank you for your warnings, but even if these rumors were

true, I would still go," he said. "My life belongs to my people, and my place is among them, and I will die when I am destined to die."

So Abdullah and Hussein set out for Jerusalem on July 20, 1951. When they arrived in the holy city, Abdullah lectured Hussein for not wearing his military uniform, the one Abdullah had given him to reward his accomplishments at Victoria College. Hussein sent a driver all the way back to Amman to pick up the uniform. He put it on and the men drove to the mosque.

Security was tight that Friday afternoon in Jerusalem. Hussein remembers seeing many armed soldiers standing beside the roadway. He asked the

Arab volunteers prepare to resist the partition of Palestine. In 1947 the United Nations divided the region into two sections, one Jewish and the other Arab, each of which was promised independence. The Arabs of Palestine (Palestinians), who constituted the majority of the population, immediately rejected the partition.

driver whether the soldiers were part of a funeral procession. They were not. When the car arrived at the mosque, a small crowd inched forward to see Jordan's king. Abdullah left the car first. Young Hussein followed behind closely. The crowd pushed toward the two men. Armed guards moved the interested spectators back. Abdullah greeted some of the onlookers while stooping to shake hands with people he recognized. As he entered the mosque, a figure emerged from behind the doors. Shukri Ashu, a fanatical Arab nationalist, aimed his gun purposefully toward Abdullah. One blast rang out. A bullet entered the king's head behind the ear and passed through his eye. Abdullah's body fell to the ground. The king was dead at Hussein's feet.

Jewish teenagers dance in the streets of New York under the newly raised flag of Israel. Israel declared itself a state independent of British rule on May 14, 1948. The United States was one of the first countries officially to recognize the new Jewish homeland.

UPI/BETTMANN NEWSPHOTOS

Arab families flee Palestine in 1948. With Israel's victory against attack by five Arab countries, half a million Arab Palestinians left their homes. Approximately half of them went to Jordan.

An Arab boy in a refugee feeding center in Damascus, Syria, in 1949. The displaced Palestinians lived in refugee camps in Syria, Lebanon, and Jordan. Most of the Arab countries, themselves poor, could barely absorb the refugees, so the Palestinians were fed and clothed primarily by United Nations relief agencies.

There was a moment of silence. Faces froze and hearts dropped. All motion and time seemed to stop. The gunman turned and began to run. Hussein instinctively followed. He trailed the assassin into a corner and suddenly found himself face to face with the murderer. Another shot exploded from the gun, this one hitting Hussein in the chest. Stunned, he fell, hit his head, and thought he was going to die. But, miraculously, the bullet hit a medal on his uniform and ricocheted. Hussein's life was spared.

AP/WIDE WORLD PHOTOS

King Abdullah in 1948. Hussein was very close to his grandfather, with whom he had long discussions about politics in the Arab world. From Abdullah, Hussein learned that "a leader's greatest duty is to serve."

3

From Schoolboy to King

The scene erupted into chaos. Abdullah's body-guards fired wildly at the assassin. The murderer's body twisted and convulsed as bullets ripped it apart. Panic overcame the crowd. Abdullah's trusted advisers scrambled for their own safety while the frightened crowd trampled the king's body. The murderer's accomplice ran away in the confusion. The king's bodyguards followed, shooting into the crowded streets of Jerusalem. Twenty people died in the rampage.

After an hour, order was restored. Abdullah's body was wrapped in a carpet and carried away. Hussein was treated for shock. The young boy stood confused and alone. His grandfather was dead, and his father, Talal, was away in Europe receiving treatment for his mental illness. Hussein realized the frailness of life. One moment Abdullah stood tall and strong, the next moment his life rushed from him and his eyes closed for the last time.

Two days later, on July 23, 1951, King Abdullah, the only leader Jordan had ever known, was buried. Five Arab nationalists were later convicted and hanged for plotting Abdullah's murder. Officially, the men were found to have acted on their own. Hussein, however, always contended that Egypt's leaders, who detested all Arabs who had friendly

I look back on my schooldays at Harrow as one of the most vital periods of my training for the responsibility I was later to assume.
—HUSSEIN
on his education at Harrow

Hussein as a student in England. After witnessing his grandfather's murder in July 1951, the young prince would have to make the transition from schoolboy to king of Jordan in little more than a year.

AP/WIDE WORLD PHOTOS

An Arab legionnaire sobs while he holds the bridle of King Abdullah's white charger during the slain ruler's funeral in Amman. Hussein always believed that Egypt was somehow involved in Abdullah's assassination.

relations with Britain, had played a role in the assassination of his grandfather.

With the king now dead, who would lead Jordan? Hussein was only 15 years old and had not yet finished school. Jordanian officials decided that Abdullah's son Naif would rule until Talal's condition improved.

Naif took to power easily. He enjoyed the feel of authority and the excitement of command. But soon after Naif assumed control, Talal regained his health. Faced with losing power, Naif desperately tried to retain the throne by dissolving Jordan's Parliament and declaring himself king. The scheme failed. Talal returned from Europe, and five British doctors declared him sane. He became king of Jordan on September 6, 1951.

Talal's coronation brought great public rejoicing. Crowds ran through the streets shouting congratulations. From windows, women made high-pitched yelps, which among Arabs expresses joy. The Jordanian people had always felt a special love for Talal. Like Abdullah, he was pure Hashemite. Both his mother and father were descended from the holy family. Naif, on the other hand, was only half Hashemite and was therefore never fully accepted. He was now exiled to a foreign country for his plot to claim the throne.

With Talal's inauguration, Hussein automatically became crown prince, the next in line for the throne. But the prince presented a problem. He still needed one year to complete his high school education and could not return to Victoria College in Egypt because of that country's suspected role in Abdullah's murder. A new school was chosen for Hussein. The choice was Harrow, a world-renowned preparatory school in Britain.

From the very first day, Hussein hated his new school. The only person he knew there was his cousin Faisal II, grandson of King Faisal of Iraq, who had died in 1933. Faisal was too young to be crowned king, and Iraq was being governed by a regent. Hussein's other classmates were unfriendly and did not speak to him. "They all had their own set of friends, and, actually, many of them seemed to me to be rather snobbish," Hussein wrote later. In the classroom, Hussein did poorly. At Harrow, people spoke English quickly, in a way Hussein did not understand. His first few weeks were spent translating rather than learning his lessons. Hussein required much tutoring and special attention to pass his courses. He disliked his new home im-

I loved my country, but I felt the responsibility of leading Jordan and serving it was far too much for me to undertake. At this time I did not want to be king.
—HUSSEIN
on the prospect of succeeding his father, Talal, as Jordan's king

41

mensely and longed for the warm sunshine of the Middle East.

The young prince persevered. He won the respect of classmates for his play in rugby. Away from school, Hussein often was seen cruising the British countryside in a sky-blue sports car. The car, a gift from the Jordanian ambassador in Britain, was fast and was excellent in turns. Hussein's cousin Faisal would often accompany the prince on Sunday drives. If Faisal couldn't go, Hussein invited one of the many pretty girls he knew. The car was the only bright spot in Hussein's unhappy time at Harrow.

In Jordan, things were equally troubled. Talal's violent fits returned, with increased severity. The king began each day feeling fine, but as the hours passed he became depressed and worried. Talal imagined that trusted friends were secretly plotting against him. As a result he dismissed many of the government's most loyal workers. In May 1952 Talal had a tantrum at a political luncheon. He smashed china and threw crystal at the diplomats. At home he beat his servants and even struck his wife, Queen Zain, whom he loved dearly. Shortly after the birth of a daughter, Talal stormed into his wife's bedroom, pulled a knife, and threatened to kill the infant to keep her from growing up in an evil world. Fortunately, a guard stopped Talal before he could harm the baby. The king later chased Hussein with a dagger, accusing the prince of being a traitor to his country.

It was a difficult time for Hussein. He loved his father and wanted him to be king. But Hussein knew that, for Jordan's sake, Talal should not remain in control. A change had to be made soon.

On August 12, 1952, while vacationing in Switzerland, Hussein heard a knock on his hotel room door. The messenger handed Hussein a telegram. It was addressed, "His Majesty, King Hussein." In accordance with Jordanian law, the country's Parliament had declared Talal incapable of ruling and had transferred power to Hussein. Hussein was now king, but only in title. He was still too young to lead the nation. In his place, a three-person council was established to govern Jordan. It ruled until Hussein took command nine months later.

Hussein made good use of the waiting period. For the first three weeks, he conducted a whirlwind tour of his country, meeting thousands of Jordanians and listening to their concerns. At one Bedouin camp, he attended a *mansef*, or Arab feast, where hundreds of men danced in a circle. They sang and fired their rifles into the dark desert sky. Hussein joined them for a while and then watched from the opening of a brown cloth tent. He thought, "With men like these, Jordan will always be secure."

It was during the tour that Hussein first flew an airplane. On a return trip to Amman, Hussein grew restless as a passenger and wandered into the airplane's cockpit. He sat in the copilot's seat and began asking the pilot questions. A long discussion followed. Hussein then asked to try the airplane's controls. The young king gently directed the plane through the high, scattered clouds. It was an exhilarating experience, one he never forgot. Hussein

Prince Hussein (left), with his uncle, Prince Naif, eight days after the death of King Abdullah. Several months later, after Naif failed in an attempt to have himself crowned king, he reluctantly handed over the throne to his brother, Talal.

Talal, father of Hussein, was crowned king of Jordan on September 6, 1951. Afflicted with bouts of schizophrenia throughout his life, Talal could not handle the pressures of ruling and was forced to step down from the throne in August 1952.

later learned to fly all types of aircraft, including jets and helicopters.

In the months before taking power, Hussein attended Sandhurst Royal Military Academy in Britain. Unlike his previous British school, Hussein enjoyed Sandhurst from the very start. The school's spit and polish style pleased him; it was full of the tradition and discipline expected in the military. He enjoyed the friendship of the many foreign students and adhered to the school's strict code of behavior. Hussein wore a uniform and awoke each morning at 5 A.M. He marched many miles in tight formation and led classmates in midnight combat exercises. Hussein studied the strategies of modern warfare and learned the procedures of command. At Sandhurst, the boy-king began to think as a soldier. He gained qualities of leadership, including confidence, pride, and a wholesome regard for adventure.

This regard stayed with Hussein throughout his life. The king was a man of action. He lived for adventure as most men live for money and power. He loved both danger and intrigue. In later wars, if the Israelis attacked a Jordanian village, Hussein was on the scene in minutes, flying his personal helicopter to the site. In war, he moved easily among his men, plotting strategy and giving encouragement. Wherever adventure beckoned, Hussein eagerly followed.

Prince Hussein (right) shakes the hand of Mukarram Jah, an Indian prince. Both are wearing the traditional "skimmer" hats of Harrow. Though unhappy at the famous English preparatory school, Hussein helped to maintain his country's good relations with Britain by finishing his high school education there.

AP/WIDE WORLD PHOTOS

King Hussein inspects an honor guard at the Sandhurst Royal Military Academy in England. Proclaimed king in August 1952, Hussein spent the months preceding his official coronation at Sandhurst, studying the strategies of modern warfare and learning the procedures of command.

AP/WIDE WORLD PHOTOS

That characteristic placed the king in the driver's seat of another car. It was a jet-black Aston-Martin, a British sports car capable of going 120 miles per hour. Hussein had wanted to race the automobile on a local track, but Jordanian officials thought this was too dangerous for their king. Instead, Hussein used the car to taxi his many friends to fancy London nightclubs.

Late one evening in the winter of 1953, after attending a club, Hussein and his friends climbed into the car. A classmate asked if he could drive back to Sandhurst. The king agreed. As they rounded a corner, the car hit an oil spot and whirled toward a lamppost. Hussein grabbed the steering wheel, and the car spun out of control and crashed through a billboard. "Change places quickly!" Hussein cried. "If anybody asks questions, remember, I was driving," the young king said. "It'll be easier."

The police soon arrived on the scene. After answering questions, the king spent several minutes chatting with the officers. By coincidence, one of the policemen had served in the police force in Palestine and had known Hussein's grandfather, Abdullah. The policeman asked the king for an autograph and then sent him on his way. Hussein's family never found out about the accident.

The incident marked the end of Hussein's carefree, schoolboy days. That spring, Hussein returned to Amman. There he accepted full powers as king of Jordan, and his life was forever changed.

King Hussein sits in an experimental model sports car at the General Motors technical center in Detroit, Michigan. Hussein spent more time driving fast cars in his early years as king than attending to the workings of his government.

4

Hussein and Nasser

Hussein awoke early on May 2, 1953. He had just returned to Jordan and now lay in bed awaiting his inauguration. Later that day he would climb the steps of his country's Parliament building and be sworn in as king. For now, however, he was content to be alone in his room contemplating the future. "From today, my life will consist of making one decision after another, all vital to Jordan," he thought. It was an awesome responsibility. He pulled the sheets to his chest and prayed he would serve his country well.

That afternoon, Hussein solemnly raised his hand skyward and said, "I swear by the name of God that I will preserve the constitution and be faithful to my people." With that, Jordan had its third king. Outside, a 101-gun salute boomed in tribute. Thousands of happy Jordanians filled the streets. They cheered and waved wildly as Hussein's motorcade drove through the narrow roads of Amman. The new king acknowledged the massive crowds with swift, precise military salutes. Later, from his palace balcony, he gave a speech. "Jordan acknowledges the brotherhood which links together all the people of the great Arab nation. Jordan is but a part of that Arab nation," he said.

Ironically, in the eastern part of that nation, another 17-year-old boy was receiving a similar reception. Hussein's cousin Faisal II became king of Iraq

> *Yesterday I could make no decisions. From today my life will consist of making one decision after another, all vital to Jordan.*
> —HUSSEIN
> the morning of his inauguration, May 2, 1953

Hussein in 1957. The young king's first years as monarch were filled with trouble and rebellion, much of it incited by Arab nationalist propaganda from Egypt and militant Palestinian groups within Jordan.

on the same day Hussein was inaugurated. Together, the new kings reaffirmed their family's ancient claim over the region. The Hashemites had faced many difficult times, but they still commanded great power, loyalty, and affection. As Hussein's mother, Queen Zain, said to the new king at his inauguration, "When you face difficulties in the future — and they're bound to come sooner or later — look back on this day. Remember then how the people of Jordan — thousands and thousands of them — showed their loyalty to you and their love and trust."

In the first two years of his reign Hussein had no time to look back; he was too busy pursuing his two favorite pastimes — cars and airplanes. During 1953 and 1954, Hussein was a young king at play. He formed an automobile club in Amman and raced against its members. One day, after driving his sports car 150 miles an hour down an abandoned airstrip, Hussein boasted, "I think she could have done better but the runway wasn't quite long enough."

The runways, however, were long enough for Hussein's daily flying lessons. During the summer of 1953, the young king was at the Amman airport five days a week. Although he took many lessons, Jordanian officials forbade him to fly alone, believing it was too dangerous. Hussein bided his time. One day, while his bodyguards were not watching, he slipped into a plane and took off alone. Hussein circled Amman and then flew off into the desert. The king's bodyguards were frantic. They had strict orders to watch Hussein closely. Fortunately, the king soon returned and, in his own words, "came in and made a perfect landing." The stunt succeeded in demonstrating that the king was a capable pilot. Hussein heard no more objections and soon learned to fly jets and helicopters. Flying was Hussein's way of escaping day-to-day pressures. "The moment I climb into a cockpit I shake off my problems and worries," he said. "Once in the air the restrictions that inevitably surround the monarchy seem to vanish. I am a man alone."

But he was not alone for long. In April 1955 he

married Dina Abdul Hamed, a beautiful and intelligent woman, also of Hashemite ancestry. Hussein respected Dina, and she bore him a daughter. But the marriage did not last. Dina was a strong-willed, complex person, with deep beliefs in Arab nationalism. Hussein, on the other hand, wanted a simple, caring wife. The marriage was a mistake; the couple never shared a true love. They separated 18 months after their wedding, and Dina left for Egypt. Their daughter, Alia, remained with Hussein in Jordan.

The king seemed untroubled by the divorce. He was soon spotted dancing with other beautiful women at fashionable nightclubs.

Hussein's busy schedule left little time for royal

A crowd gathers outside the parliament building in Amman to greet Jordan's new monarch. Hussein was inaugurated as Jordan's third king on May 2, 1953.

51

Hussein's cousin Faisal II became king of Iraq the same day Hussein was inaugurated in Jordan. The two Hashemite princes had attended Harrow together, and their personal bonds of loyalty and affection ensured close political ties between Jordan and Iraq.

UPI/BETTMANN NEWSPHOTOS

The British refused to give us ammunition but they agreed to send barbed wire.

—GENERAL J. B. GLUBB describing the British policy of supporting a defensive rather than offensive position by Jordan's army

duties, but he was unconcerned. He let others run the army. General Glubb and a group of British officers kept the West Bank Palestinians under control with armed patrols. Glubb also worked to strengthen Jordan's border with Israel. Other advisers decided how to spend the British money that supported Jordan's economy. Hussein showed up at his office irregularly and was late for many important meetings. He also demonstrated little understanding of Middle Eastern politics. Once, while touring his country's 400-mile border with Israel, he asked General Glubb why Jordan could not attack the Jewish state. Glubb politely reminded the king that Jordan's army of 20,000 soldiers was no match for Israel's 250,000-man army. Hussein, however, was too preoccupied to learn such details. He was a race-car driver, fighter pilot, and playboy. It was for other people to worry about running the government.

While Hussein played, others plotted in his poor country. In the early 1950s two-thirds of Jordan's population still was without permanent homes. Since the war with Israel, Jordan's Palestinian refugees had remained in tent camps living off food rations that cost nine cents a day. They had no work and sat idly as Israelis farmed land they once owned. Under these dismal conditions, their hatred grew. The Palestinians blamed Britain, which supported Israel, for their miserable existence. They also condemned Hussein, who still depended on the British for financial and military support. The Palestinians were a people without an identity, and they were looking for a leader.

That leadership came in the form of Gamal Abdel Nasser, president of Egypt. Nasser came to power

Twenty-one-year-old King Hussein goes for a ride in a British jet plane. His passion for flying helicopters and jets was Hussein's way of escaping the day-to-day pressures of life as a ruler in the turbulent Middle East.

AP/WIDE WORLD PHOTOS

Palestinian refugees in 1957. In the early 1950s Jordan's Palestinians, who lived in terrible poverty, made up two-thirds of the country's population. They became increasingly resentful of Hussein, who, they felt, was not doing enough to fight Israel.

in July 1952, after the overthrow of King Farouk. He was a popular figure in the Middle East because of his near-fanatical devotion to Arab nationalism. Nasser dreamed of a unified Arab state, free from outside influence, but his Arab state had its center in Egypt. He backed his dream with an army equipped with the latest Soviet-made weapons and machinery.

Nasser was also a master of spreading untruths. He skillfully manipulated Egyptian newspapers and radio to sway public opinion in other Arab states. Each day, Palestinian refugees living in Jordan listened as Egyptian radio warned of growing British influence in the Middle East. Nasser campaigned vigorously against Britain's "evil hand" of control. The untruths were well received by the Palestinians, who saw Nasser as a hero of the Arab cause.

Palestinian unrest was further incited by Iraq and Turkey's signing of the Baghdad Pact in February 1955. The Baghdad Pact was an agreement designed to prevent the Soviet Union from extending its influence in the Middle East. Iraq and Turkey agreed that if either was attacked, presumably by the Soviet Union, they would come to each other's defense. The British strongly supported the agreement, which was interpreted by the Arabs as another example of British interference in the Middle East. Nasser was particularly outraged. He considered the pact a serious blow to Arab nationalism. Nasser reasoned that if Iraq was bound to Turkey, which was not an Arab country, it would not be free to join with the other Arab states in forming a single nation. He became even more incensed when Britain joined the Baghdad Pact in April 1955.

A war of words soon followed, pitting Egypt against Iraq. Egyptian radio condemned Iraq's King Faisal for bending to British pressure. "The aim of the alliance is to destroy Arabism in Palestine," Cairo radio blared. "Down with the Baghdad Pact. Join with Nasser," the newspaper headlines read. To complicate matters, Nasser made a huge military deal with the Soviet Union in September 1955. He now owned a great arsenal of tanks and military hardware.

When I consider these hundreds of millions [of Muslims] united by a single creed, I emerge with a sense of the tremendous possibilities which we might realize through concerted action with all these Muslims . . . enabling them and their brothers in faith to wield power wisely and without limit.
—GAMAL ABDEL NASSER
president of Egypt

AP/WIDE WORLD PHOTOS

**King Farouk of Egypt in
1947. Farouk's government,
riddled with corruption and
blamed for Egypt's defeat by
Israel in 1948, was over-
thrown in 1952 by a military
junta. The power behind the
coup was Gamal Abdel Nas-
ser, a fiery Arab nationalist.**

In the middle of this power struggle was Hussein.
On the one hand, he owed personal allegiance to his
cousin Faisal and to the British, who still gave his
country $35 million a year. On the other hand, he
agreed with some of Nasser's views about Arab nationalism. He also was disappointed that Iraq had
not consulted with other Arab countries before joining the pact.

At the same time, Britain was pressuring Jordan to join the Baghdad Pact. The British believed that Jordan's membership in the pact would protect British interests in the area. A British general secretly met with Hussein to negotiate Jordan's acceptance of the pact. The talks took weeks. The British offered increased financial and military support if Hussein signed. They also agreed to promote Arabs to high ranks in the British-run Jordanian army, a move Hussein staunchly supported.

Somehow, Nasser learned about the secret negotiations. He was outraged that Hussein would

Egyptians holding up signs bearing anti-Western, pro-Russian slogans cheer President Nasser in Cairo in 1956. Nasser increased Egypt's military strength through arms deals with the Soviets and, through a relentless Radio Cairo propaganda campaign, aroused Palestinian sentiment against Hussein.

King Hussein meets with President Nasser in 1957. Increased tension between Jordan and Egypt had been mounting since 1955 when, in secret negotiations, Britain put pressure on Hussein to sign the anti-Soviet Baghdad Pact. Nasser denounced Hussein's dealings with the British as traitorous to the Arab nationalist cause.

think of joining the pact. Nasser had always considered Hussein a weak leader. "He's a nice kid. But he should be back in school rather than in Amman running a country," Nasser once said. With those sentiments, Nasser turned his massive propaganda machine against the king. Throughout the fall of 1955, Egyptian radio unleashed a relentless campaign against the king and the British officers who led his army. Radio announcers called Hussein a traitor to the Arab cause and a puppet of General Glubb. Palestinians listening in Jordan picked up the message. Palestinian schoolteachers even

taught their pupils anti-Hussein slogans and sent them to the streets to create trouble. Adults followed, chanting against the government. The demonstrations soon turned violent. Angry mobs burned cars and stoned government buildings.

Hussein acted quickly. He used his army to restore peace. The soldiers fired tear gas into the crowds and arrested protesters. A 10-day curfew was imposed. The riots continued into early 1956. Order eventually was restored but the protests succeeded. Hussein never signed the Baghdad Pact, and his political image was seriously damaged. In his first important act as king, Hussein turned his army on the Palestinians living in Jordan. Arabs throughout the Middle East condemned Hussein's use of force. They wondered if Nasser was not correct in calling Hussein a traitor to the Arab world. Hussein was now in very serious trouble with his Arab neighbors.

One of the Arab tank crews sent by Hussein to put down anti-Western riots in Amman in 1955. The king used the army to stop violent demonstrations by Palestinians in Jordan, who were protesting reports that Hussein planned to join the Baghdad Pact defense alliance.

5
Threats From All Sides

The Baghdad Pact riots had ended, but the consequences of the violent protests lingered in Jordan during the first two months of 1956. Nasser continued his verbal attack on Hussein and his government. The Palestinians listened and became angrier. Jordan became more tense and serious.

Hussein also became more somber. After the riots, the young king spent less time racing cars and flying planes, and turned his attention to royal duties and responsibilities. In response to Nasser's verbal attacks, Hussein made a dramatic move. In March 1956 the king dismissed General Glubb as chief of staff of Jordan's army.

Glubb's contribution to Jordan's history was great. He arrived there in 1930 to settle violent disputes between warring Bedouin tribes. Hussein's grandfather, Abdullah, had been impressed with Glubb's handling of the situation and soon placed the young British officer in charge of Jordan's army. Glubb served Abdullah well. At a time when most Arab armies fought on horseback with swords, Glubb developed a highly disciplined fighting force of 20,000 men. This crack unit was the envy of the Arab world. By 1956 Jordan's army owned an impressive collection of very sophisticated military equipment.

Hussein, however, never shared his grandfather's

We are Arabs first and Jordanians second. As Jordanians, we have learned one lesson that contributes daily to our progress: we have clarity of purpose. Having escaped death as a nation, we must make our life as a nation worth living.
—HUSSEIN

In 1963 Hussein addresses a group of his followers who had gathered at the royal palace to pledge their support. The loyalty of the military, especially the Bedouin soldiers, was a crucial factor in Hussein's maintaining power during the tumultuous 1950s and 1960s.

UPI/BETTMANN NEWSPHOTOS

affection for Glubb. The king appreciated Glubb's accomplishments but questioned his place in the country's future. "Jordan is a young and impetuous country, and we were, and still are, in more of a hurry than Glubb was to achieve our national aims," Hussein later wrote in 1962. Glubb was a conservative soldier, who based his military strategy on the defense of Jordan against an Israeli attack. This contrasted dramatically with Hussein's desire to someday launch a military offensive against Israel.

Adding to the problem was Egyptian propaganda. Glubb had become a focal point of Nasser's lies. Egyptian radio ran incorrect reports of how Glubb, not Hussein, ruled Jordan. To many Arabs, Glubb became a symbol of the hated British influence in the Middle East.

Hussein believed it best to dispose of Glubb cleanly and abruptly. The king gave Glubb only one day to pack his belongings and leave the country he had served for 26 years.

The move worked. The announcement of Glubb's discharge on March 1, 1956, set off wild rejoicing throughout the Middle East. Arab nationalists praised Hussein for standing up to the British government. They believed Glubb's removal was an important step toward further independence from British influence.

The British, however, were less enthusiastic. They were angered by Hussein's hasty move and threatened to stop giving money to Jordan. Hussein acted quickly to calm their displeasure. He met with British officials and assured them that Jordan's friendship with Britain remained intact. British soldiers could remain on Jordanian soil. Likewise, Hussein expected Britain to continue paying support. The British soon accepted the situation. It was a major political victory for Hussein. The young king had quieted his Arab neighbors without losing British monetary support.

But there was little time to savor his success. Events were already unfolding that would dramatically affect the young king's life.

The period after Glubb's discharge was a time of experimentation in Jordan. Hussein made sweep-

For many years our leaders had ceased to think of Jordan as a country standing alone; in any crisis it had become axiomatic to go to the British ambassador for advice.
—HUSSEIN

General John Bagot Glubb after his dismissal as British commander of the Jordanian army. In March 1956 Hussein dismissed the general, who had served the country since 1930, in an effort to placate anti-British sentiment in Jordan.

ing changes throughout the country. "I had felt deeply that Jordanian political leaders had relied too much and overlong on outside help," Hussein recalled. "I decided, therefore, that younger and more promising politicians and army officers should have a chance to show their mettle." Hussein acted swiftly. He promoted Arabs to ranks in the army formerly held only by the British. One promotion went to Ali Abu Nuwar. Hussein had known Nuwar for many years and respected his cool demeanor. Nuwar had worked for Jordan as a military attaché in France and had served under Glubb in the Jordanian army. Hussein promoted him to chief of staff, the job General Glubb had once held.

In the government, changes similar to those occurring in the army were beginning. In October 1956 Jordan held a parliamentary election that resulted in Arab National Socialists and communists winning many seats. The two groups were a dangerous combination. Both were radical and prone to violence, and both were working for the dissolution of Jordan into a greater unified Arab state. On October 27, 1956, the new Parliament elected Suleiman Nabulsi prime minister. Nabulsi was an Arab nationalist and close friend of Ali Abu Nuwar.

Until Nabulsi's election, Jordan's prime ministers had answered to the king. Nabulsi, however, contended that Jordan's constitution only held him accountable to the country's Parliament. Consequently, Hussein held little control over Nabulsi.

For example, when Israel attacked Egypt to begin the Sinai War of October 1956, Hussein ordered an

Ali Abu Nuwar was appointed army chief of staff in June 1956 as part of Hussein's efforts to promote Jordanians to the highest positions in the army and government. Nuwar's extreme Arab nationalism, however, helped foster antiroyalist sentiment in the military.

immediate military strike against Israel. Nabulsi canceled the order, declaring it "ridiculous" that Hussein would assume the authority to order a strike. Jordan stayed out of the altercation. This military action was undertaken by Israel in response to Nasser's nationalization of the Suez Canal, the waterway connecting the Red Sea to the Mediterranean Sea. The canal was essential to all trade between Europe and Asia. Great Britain and France supported Israel, believing that leaving the canal completely in Nasser's control was dangerous.

The war lasted only nine days. The United Nations intervened and a truce was soon declared. Multinational peacekeeping forces moved in to maintain peace in the area.

The Suez crisis further solidified anti-British sentiment in Jordan. In November 1956 Jordan's Parliament, which supported Nasser, voted to end the country's long-standing friendship with Britain and to open relations with the Soviet Union. To replace the money Britain had supplied, Jordan signed the Arab Solidarity Agreement with Egypt, Syria, and Saudi Arabia. The three countries promised to pay Jordan large sums of money for its rejection of British aid.

The tone was set. Jordan was moving decisively away from Britain's moderate influence and toward the extreme leftist philosophies of Arab nationalism. Nabulsi allowed radical nationalists to enter the government. Nuwar converted many members of Jordan's army to the Arab nationalist cause. Hussein was helpless. Neither Nabulsi nor Nuwar obeyed him. The government and army were turning against the king. A military overthrow looked certain. "It is doubtful Jordan will last out the year as an independent state," a *New York Times* reporter wrote in February 1957.

But people underestimated the young king's resolve. On April 10, 1957, Hussein dismissed Nabulsi as prime minister. It was a legal but dangerous act. Nabulsi was Jordan's first freely elected prime minister and was supported firmly throughout Jordan. Street riots immediately broke out in Amman. Palestinians on the West Bank began violent protests.

The Nabulsi government is a singular phenomenon in the history of Jordan. It was a cabinet, the senior members of which rejected the "image of Jordan" — consciously and publicly — point by point. The Hashemite tradition was nothing to them; the king, if permitted to reign, should certainly not rule.
—URIEL DANN
historian

United Nations peacekeeping troops in the Gaza Strip. In the summer of 1956, Egypt nationalized the Suez Canal. To free the canal, Israel attacked Egypt, capturing much of the Sinai peninsula. The UN sent a multinational force to occupy the land that had been taken by Israel and to act as a buffer between Egypt and Israel.

Extremist groups of all kinds demonstrated against the king.

Hussein tried to regain control by establishing a more moderate government. But before he could act, Nuwar issued an ultimatum. Either Hussein form a government partial to Arab nationalism or Nuwar would turn Jordan's army against the king. The situation seemed hopeless. Nuwar controlled the military.

Just then, the king was visited by a soldier in the Jordanian army. The soldier told Hussein that many Bedouins in the army remained loyal and were ready to fight to preserve the kingdom in the event of a coup attempt. Hussein asked the soldier to return to his outfit and tell no one about his meeting with the king.

Hussein then called in Nuwar to confront him with his knowledge of the commander's intentions. But before the meeting began, there was a telephone call for Nuwar. It was from Nuwar's co-conspirator in Zerqa, a large military base northeast of Amman. The caller told Nuwar that Bedouin soldiers loyal to the king had learned of the planned coup and had revolted against their officers. The Bedouin troops, fearful for Hussein's life, were preparing to march on Amman to save their king and kill Nuwar.

Hussein overheard the discussion and grabbed the telephone receiver. "I'll be right over!" the king shouted. Hussein then jumped into his car and headed for Zerqa. He wanted to meet his men and personally calm their fears. It was a brash move. Hussein had no idea of the danger ahead.

The scene at Zerqa was chaotic. Half-dressed men darted through the dark desert night yelling hysterically. Jordanian soldiers, believing their king's life was in danger, shot at one another in vain at-

Hussein and Nasser shake hands after the signing of the "Aid to Jordan" pact in Cairo in January 1957. In the treaty, Egypt, Saudi Arabia, and Syria agreed to provide an annual $35 million to replace Jordan's military subsidy from the British.

UPI/BETTMANN NEWSPHOTOS

tempts to kill traitors. When Hussein's car arrived, it was greeted by soldiers pointing submachine guns. The king quickly emerged from the car and showed his face. "I am Hussein," he shouted. "I am all right. My life is yours. All is well. Back to your camps."

The men immediately laid down their weapons and pledged him their loyalty. Festivities ensued throughout the night celebrating the king's survival. Hussein would come upon a group of angry soldiers, leave his car, and talk to the men, winning their affection. Occasionally, heavy gunfire rang out as the king spoke. But Hussein continued his rounds for many hours, and by night's end, he had restored order.

In the next two weeks Hussein imposed harsh military control over the country. Curfews were ordered and military courts tried civilian protesters. The rebellious Nuwar was exiled from Jordan. By May 1957 peace had returned. Hussein had defeated Arab nationalists within Jordan.

In other parts of the Middle East, the call for a unified Arab nation continued. Nasser won followings in Syria and Saudi Arabia. In fact, on February 1, 1958, Egypt and Syria formally joined to create the United Arab Republic (U.A.R.), a union dominated by Nasser. In response to Nasser's formation of the United Arab Republic, Jordan and Iraq joined to form the Arab Union on February 14. According to Hussein, this agreement was "based on absolute equality; it was an attempt at a model union between two states. It constituted the first realistic, idealistic step toward the fuller, more comprehensive Arab unity." The Arab Union was a mutual defense agreement against the growing threat of communism in the Middle East. Hussein later wrote, "Both of us [Hussein and Faisal II] believed passionately in the real Arab freedom for which our great-grandfather had fought. Here was a real opportunity to show the Arab world how a constitutional democratic system of government could operate between two united, progressive states." The head of the Arab Union would be Faisal, with Hussein as his deputy. The future of this new ar-

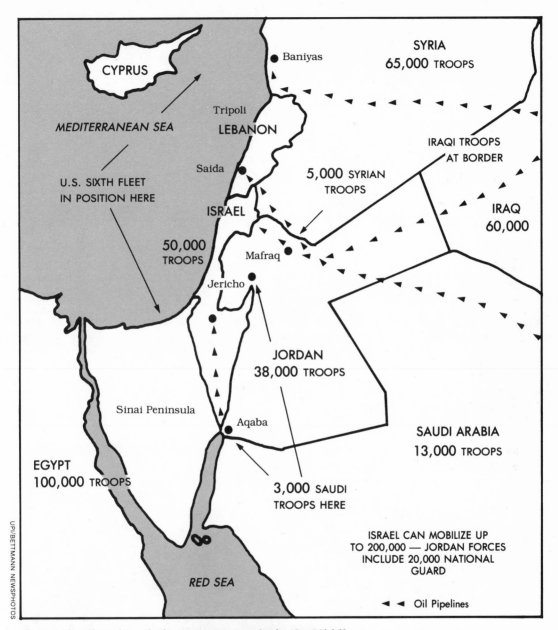

CYPRUS

MEDITERRANEAN SEA

U.S. SIXTH FLEET
IN POSITION HERE

Baniyas

Tripoli

LEBANON

SYRIA
65,000 TROOPS

Saida

ISRAEL

50,000
TROOPS

5,000 SYRIAN
TROOPS

IRAQI TROOPS
AT BORDER

IRAQ
60,000

Mafraq

Jericho

JORDAN
38,000 TROOPS

Sinai Peninsula

Aqaba

SAUDI ARABIA
13,000 TROOPS

EGYPT
100,000 TROOPS

3,000 SAUDI
TROOPS HERE

ISRAEL CAN MOBILIZE UP
TO 200,000 — JORDAN FORCES
INCLUDE 20,000 NATIONAL
GUARD

RED SEA

◄ ◄ Oil Pipelines

A map showing the relative troop strengths in the Middle
East in 1957. In April of that year an attempt was made
by Nuwar and other pro-Nasser officers to take over the
government and the large military base at Zerqa. Hussein, rallying his loyal troops, declared martial law and
prepared to fight for his throne. Note the presence of the
U.S. Sixth Fleet in the eastern Mediterranean, ready to
offset any move made by the Soviet Union in the region.

rangement looked positive. However, Nasser and the United Arab Republic were not pleased with this rival Arab nation and decided to take severe measures against its continuance.

In Baghdad, Iraq, Arab nationalists, backed by the U.A.R., brutally murdered King Faisal and took control of the government on July 14, 1958. The assassination carried both emotional and political consequences for Hussein. He loved his cousin deeply. They had attended Harrow together and had shared many happy moments. Politically, the murder destroyed the Arab Union and effectively isolated Jordan. On its borders sat Egypt, Syria, Saudi Arabia, and Iraq, which were all fiercely opposed to Hussein because of his position on Arab nationalism. The four Arab countries called for an economic boycott of Jordan. They blockaded roads and closed their airspace to Jordanian planes. Jordan quickly ran low on food and oil. Supplies were rationed and travel was restricted. Conditions worsened as the

A Bedouin of the Jordanian Camel Corps practices his sharpshooting while his camel hugs the ground beside him. During the Zerqa riots, Bedouin troops had prepared to march on the capital to save Hussein from Nuwar's planned coup.

entire country ground to a halt. Jordan's survival was seriously threatened.

But Hussein had learned well from previous adversity. The king was not to be easily defeated. Shortly after Faisal's assassination, Hussein had issued an urgent plea for help to Britain and the United States. The king explained the seriousness of the situation and the need for immediate aid. Both countries responded generously. Britain sent troops. The Americans flew in oil and food. Jordan was saved, but it was a humiliating rescue. By accepting British military aid, Hussein again had to rely on a foreign country to solve his problems. Moreover, because the Americans flew their supplies over Israeli airspace, it looked like Israel was tacitly supporting Jordan.

In his autobiography, published in 1962, Hussein never expressed any gratitude toward Israel for helping to defeat the Arab blockade of Jordan. His Arab neighbors contended that the action was another example of Hussein clinging to power at any cost. When threatened from inside his country, the king turned to the military. When the threat was from the outside, he accepted help from anyone, even Israel, the Arabs' most hated enemy.

Members of the British "Red Devils" parachute regiment relax after their arrival in Jordan from Cyprus. After the assassination by Arab nationalists of his cousin King Faisal of Iraq in July 1958, Hussein asked for British and American protection from any plot to bring down his regime, a move that further alienated him from the other Arab nations.

> *Ours was everything a union between friendly states should be; a fortnight previously, Egypt and Syria had formed the United Arab Republic — in my opinion, everything a union of states should not be.*
> —HUSSEIN
> comparing the Iraq-Jordan Arab Union to the United Arab Republic

6

Prosperity Gives Way to Defeat

After Faisal's death, numerous attempts were made on Hussein's life. In fact, Hussein began carrying a submachine gun to protect himself. The two most bizarre plots against Hussein's life occurred in the summer of 1960. The king was having sinus trouble and carried a bottle of nose drops wherever he went. One evening, while the king was visiting a friend, one of his assistants accidentally spilled some of the drops from the bottle into a sink. The liquid bubbled and frothed before burning deep pits in the porcelain. The fluid was acid. An investigation showed that a servant to Hussein had placed the acid in the bottle to kill the king.

Even more strange was the case of the dead cats. "Amman abounds with cats," Hussein wrote. "My grandfather loved cats, and a large floating cat population on the palace grounds has always been tolerated." While walking on the palace grounds, Hussein noticed three dead cats. At first, he thought the poor cats had just starved. On his way to summon servants to bury the cats, he happened to tell a guard of his discovery. The man immediately became suspicious. Six other cats had already been found dead. An inquiry revealed that Arab nationalists had bribed the king's assistant cook to poison Hussein's food. Unsure of the required dosage, the

> *I have a simple philosophy about life and death. How easily it comes and how easily it can end! What man can afford to waste time? At any moment death can claim anyone, and when it does, death is unimportant. The only thing that matters is the work that one has accomplished.*
> —HUSSEIN

King Hussein eats his lunch in the field as he views damage to a village in the Jordan Valley following a battle between Jordanian and Israeli forces in February 1968.

AP/WIDE WORLD PHOTOS

cook had experimented on the palace's cats.

Hussein was undaunted by the ill-fated attempts. Through luck and instinct, the king had displayed an uncanny ability to escape danger. "I fear only God," he once told a group of reporters. Unaffected by the scheming, the king continued to perform his royal duties with increasing skill and commitment. Under Hussein's leadership, Jordan showed remarkable progress and stability during the early 1960s. Its Arab neighbors, caught in their own problems, eased their harsh criticism of Hussein. Likewise, the strict laws enacted by the king after the Zerqa riots of 1957 kept West Bank Palestinians firmly under control.

The new climate allowed Hussein to improve his impoverished desert country. Although still dependent on British and American financial support, Jordan's economy prospered. Crop production increased significantly thanks to an irrigation project that turned 75,000 acres of desert into lush gardens of fruits and vegetables. Oil refineries and factories were built. Palestinians who had been merchants before the war with Israel again began trading goods. The wealth of the nation and its people increased. Many schools opened, including the country's first college, the University of Jordan, in 1962. Jordan seemed a far happier place than at any time in its recent past.

The happiness spilled over into Hussein's personal life. In the spring of 1960 Hussein met a young British woman whose father was an officer stationed in Jordan. They became close friends and were seen together frequently. Her name was Toni Gardiner and she was a caring, unpretentious woman. They fell in love and were married on May 25, 1961. It was a simple ceremony. Toni converted to Islam and changed her name to Muna al-Hussein, or "Hussein's wish." The couple had four children, two boys and twin girls. They lived a quiet life, full of easy pleasures. The marriage filled a void in Hussein's personal life. Shortly after the wedding, Hussein wrote, "I am at ease. I am happy. I finally have a home." Publicly, the union improved Hussein's royal image. He was now accepted as a committed

family man. His adventure-seeking playboy days seemed long gone.

Hussein also won respect in other parts of the Middle East. Arab nationalists in Egypt, Syria, and Saudi Arabia began to appreciate the king for his many accomplishments and abundant courage. Hussein had faced many difficult situations. A lesser man would have broken under the years of pressure and strife. Yet Hussein overcame the adversities, and, in true Arab fashion, became even stronger and more determined with each obstacle he conquered.

This hard-won confidence accompanied Hussein to an important Arab summit conference in January 1964. There, he met face-to-face with other Arab leaders, who accepted him as their equal. The conference resulted in a monumental resolution that even today greatly affects Middle Eastern politics. The resolution established the Palestine Liberation

Arab nationalists on trial in Amman in 1958, accused of attempting to kill King Hussein with bombs. Hussein, though always heavily protected by bodyguards, was lucky to survive several attempts on his life.

Organization, or PLO, and gave it responsibility for Palestinian resistance against Israel. Hussein supported the idea, believing it would channel Palestinian energies in a positive direction. "We wanted the PLO to be a mirror reflecting the unity of Arab Palestine — a catalyst for its energies, an organization that would harness all Palestinians' vital forces," Hussein said in 1969. The king stipulated, however, that the PLO in Jordan had to cooperate fully with Jordanian officials and could not interfere with the internal affairs of his country. The conference ended on friendly terms, but the violent consequences of PLO involvement in the Middle East would last for many years to come.

The first consequences were felt in the mid-1960s. After the Arab summit conference, the PLO established offices in Amman and on the West Bank. There it recruited soldiers and soon tried to collect taxes to finance an army. This angered Hussein. He thought the PLO's increasing activities intruded on Jordan's rights as a free nation.

The PLO also supported terrorist acts against Israel. At night, PLO soldiers sneaked into Israel along Jordan's long and unguarded border. There they killed livestock, destroyed property, and often murdered Israeli farmers. Hussein opposed the acts, believing they would cause a war with Israel that Jordan could not win. But the PLO persisted and the frequency of the raids increased through 1966. Finally, on November 13, 1966, Israel retaliated by attacking the Jordanian village of Samu and destroying homes believed to shelter PLO terrorists. The Jordanian army responded to the attack by sending troops, but the soldiers were ambushed by the Israelis on the outskirts of Samu. In all, 21 Jordanians died and 31 were injured in the violence.

Israel's action set off massive demonstrations in Palestinian communities. Organized by the PLO, the protests were the most violent Jordan had ever witnessed. Outrage was directed at Israel and Hussein, who was blamed for denying the PLO the right to arm and defend itself.

The demonstrations soon attracted the attention of Hussein's old enemies. Arab nationalists in Egypt

Water being extracted from wells as deep as 250 feet at
Wadi Ram, near Amman. As the early 1960s brought relative peace to Jordan, Hussein turned to domestic economic issues. Irrigation projects such as this one helped
Jordan's crop production and promoted general welfare.

King Hussein married his second wife, Toni Gardiner, on May 25, 1961. Daughter of a British army officer, Gardiner converted to Islam and subsequently changed her name to Muna al-Hussein, or "Hussein's wish."

and Syria broke their long silence and raised their voices against Israel and Jordan.

It was an extremely difficult time for Hussein. Like his Arab brothers, he dreamed of someday driving the Jews from Palestine. But as a soldier, he knew the time was not right. Arab interests were too divided to launch a successful attack. The Arab governments shared little communication and had no organized battle plan. Hussein believed that an immediate move against Israel would be disastrous.

No one listened to the young king, however. On May 16, 1967, Egyptian President Nasser told the United Nations to remove its peacekeeping force from the Sinai peninsula. The force had acted as a buffer between Egypt and Israel since 1958. The troops left, and Nasser quickly blockaded Israel's southern ports and advanced his army to the Israeli border.

Hussein realized that war was close at hand. "From the day the United Nations troops were withdrawn, I foresaw the consequences of this decision,"

King Hussein with his sons by Muna, Prince Abdullah and Prince Faisal. This period in the king's life marked a change in Hussein's image from playboy to family man.

A battle scene from the 1967 Six-Day War. After the United Nations withdrew its peacekeeping force from the Sinai peninsula in May 1967, Egypt moved its army to the Israeli border. On June 7, Israel attacked Egypt, and Hussein, bound by a mutual defense agreement, joined in the war against Israel.

Hussein once said in an interview. "To me it was obvious. War with Israel was inevitable." Jordan's involvement was also certain. The Palestinians had made it clear: either Hussein join them or risk full-scale civil war within Jordan. Hussein decided to join the fight against Israel. But first he needed to find support.

For many years, Hussein knew that Jordan was vulnerable to an Israeli attack. Jordan's army was small. The country's long border with Israel had few defensible positions. Hussein reasoned that if an Arab-Israeli war occurred, Jordan would be the most likely target of an Israeli attack. To lessen this possibility, the king met with Nasser and signed a controversial defense pact. The two men agreed that Jordan and Egypt would fight together against any threat from Israel.

From that point on, events broke quickly. Realizing war was imminent, Israel took the offensive position and attacked Egypt on June 7, 1967. Hussein learned of the situation that morning and drove to Jordanian army headquarters. Details were sketchy, but Nasser confirmed the attack and claimed to have destroyed three-quarters of the Israeli air force. It was a lie. Egypt had suffered great losses and its military had been crippled.

On the misinformation, Hussein's army entered the fighting. Jordan began shelling Israeli towns. Jordanian tanks and war planes were sent into battle. The hasty action was a major mistake. If Hussein had stayed out of the fighting for an additional day, the full extent of Egypt's defeat would have been known and Jordan's army could have been saved from destruction. It was not to be, however. Characteristically, Hussein acted rashly. The Israelis answered forcefully. In the six days of fighting, Israel's

Israeli soldiers standing next to a captured antiaircraft gun watch Egyptian positions on the opposite side of the Suez Canal. Nasser claimed that Egypt inflicted heavy losses on the Israelis, but in reality, the Egyptians had been rapidly beaten back by Israel.

army captured the Sinai peninsula from Egypt, the Golan Heights from Syria, and the West Bank from Jordan. Moreover, the combined Arab armies were completely ruined. Jordan alone lost more than 6,000 men, most of its tanks, and all of its air force.

Israel's victory in the Six-Day War was one of the quickest, most effective military operations in the history of modern warfare. Its success was due to superior training and better organization. The Israelis also fought with the strongest conviction. Unlike the Arabs, they acted out of self-preservation. If they lost, their country would cease to exist. The Arabs, however, fought for the Palestinians. They felt less of the common spirit and commitment that bound the Israelis.

Throughout the war, Hussein stayed close to the fighting. He drove in a jeep from one army unit to another, offering support and encouragement. It

King Hussein and his soldiers practice with rifles on a firing range. Hussein stayed close to his troops during the Six-Day War through some of the toughest fighting on the West Bank. In a crushing defeat, Jordan lost 6,000 men and most of its tanks, and its air force was annihilated.

was sorely needed. Jordan's troops were at the complete mercy of Israel's army. Jordanian soldiers were battered by artillery, harassed by air fire, and bombarded by tank assaults. The defeat left an indelible image in Hussein's mind. "I will never forget the hallucinating sight of that defeat," he said in 1967. "Roads clogged with trucks, jeeps, and all kinds of vehicles twisted, disemboweled, dented, still smoking, giving off that particular smell of metal and paint burned by exploding bombs — a stink that only powder can make." The war was a crushing and humiliating experience. All Hussein could now do was pick up the pieces.

Palestinian recruits serving with a civil defense unit in the Gaza Strip in May 1967. The Palestinians are shouting, "We want to fight. We will take back our homeland. Palestine is Arab."

7

A Country Divided

Hussein required many months to fully comprehend the consequences of his country's defeat. Jordan had lost much in the fighting. Many of the country's most courageous men were now dead. The important historical cities of Bethlehem, Jerusalem, and Jericho were surrendered during the war. Economically, the country lost to the Israelis much productive farmland and many prosperous towns and villages. Jordan was now poorer, less stable, and virtually defenseless as a result of the war. Its army was battered and its border with Israel was pushed east to the Jordan River. "Our calamity is greater than anyone could have imagined," the king announced after the battle.

The war also had a devastating effect on Hussein. The king's self-assured style disappeared. He wept openly to his advisers and was often depressed. He rarely saw his family and was hospitalized for facial pain and heart trouble. The late 1960s were the most difficult years of Hussein's life.

The king faced even more problems. Forced from their West Bank homes, Palestinian refugees now moved east into the heartland of Jordan. There they settled in hastily built tent camps in Amman and other major cities.

In such close proximity to the king, the Palestinians at first tried to work with Hussein. But old

Any hand raised against this united and struggling nation will be cut off, and any eye which looks at us with a look of hatred will be gouged out.
—HUSSEIN
responding to threats made
by the Palestine Liberation
Organization in 1966

King Hussein with a self-loading rifle as he visits commando troops in June 1970. During the late 1960s, Palestinian activity in Jordan grew increasingly militant. By September 1970, Jordanian army troops were engaged in a life-or-death struggle with Palestinian guerrillas for control of the country.

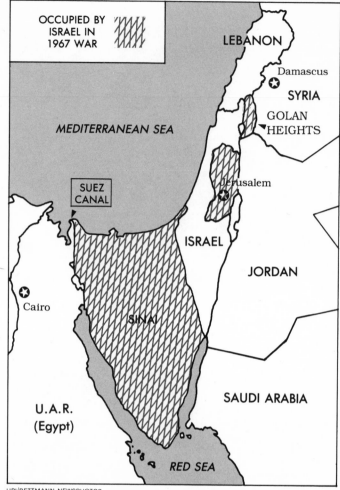

OCCUPIED BY
ISRAEL IN
1967 WAR

LEBANON

Damascus

SYRIA

GOLAN
HEIGHTS

MEDITERRANEAN SEA

SUEZ
CANAL

Jerusalem

ISRAEL

JORDAN

Cairo

SINAI

SAUDI ARABIA

U.A.R.
(Egypt)

RED SEA

This map shows the territories occupied by Israel in the 1967 Six-Day War. Israel captured the Gaza Strip and the Sinai peninsula from Egypt, the Golan Heights from Syria, and the West Bank from Jordan. Israel expanded its territory to three times what it had been before the war.

differences soon surfaced. The PLO reemerged as a major political force. It organized an army, distributed guns, and acted independently of the Jordanian government. The PLO had its own laws and courts, collected taxes, and even registered cars under their own rules.

Through 1968 and 1969, militant Palestinian activity increased. Armed with Soviet weapons, the Palestinians established army training camps in the desert and flaunted guns in Jordan's streets. Lawlessness became a way of life as the *fedayeen*, Arab commandos, claimed large areas within Jordan.

Yet Hussein avoided confrontations. His country

and its people had suffered much during the war of 1967. Hussein believed the Jordanians deserved peace, and he worked toward that goal by meeting with PLO representatives and exploring nonviolent methods of quelling the unrest.

The PLO, however, was set on war. They remained fiercely committed to the complete destruction of Israel and were unable to accept any alternative. Frustrated by improved border defenses, PLO commandos could no longer vent their anger by waging

An Arab woman weeps as she prepares to leave her home on the West Bank of the Jordan river in Israeli-occupied territory. Thousands of refugees poured into Jordan and settled in tent camps in Amman and other cities.

An Arab youth stands at attention in his guerrilla training camp on the outskirts of Amman. The Palestine Liberation Organization, the commando army dedicated to retaking Palestine from the Israelis, established these training camps in the desert, virtually setting up its own government within Jordan.

night raids on Israel. Instead, their violent activities were restricted to the poor country of Jordan. By 1970 Amman was an armed camp. Guns and weapons were everywhere. PLO soldiers stopped Jordanian citizens at will. Anyone not supporting their cause was harassed and tormented. Even Hussein was subjected to the violence when his motorcade came under PLO attack in June 1970. The vehicles were stopped at a routine army roadblock when the ambush occurred. At the sound of gunfire, Hussein's bodyguards scrambled to the roadside and shot in the direction of the attack. Hussein, however, remained in his car, firing wildly out a side window. He finally came to his senses and crawled out of the car to safety. The shooting continued until the king's guards overpowered the rebels. One Jordanian soldier was killed and eight Palestinians were mortally wounded.

Word of the assassination attempt quickly spread through Jordan's army. Bedouin soldiers were outraged by the boldness of the Palestinian assault. They waited for Hussein's orders to attack PLO positions. None came, however. Hussein still believed a peaceful solution could be achieved.

Then, on September 6, 1970, the PLO struck again in spectacular fashion. Late in the day, Palestinian commandos hijacked three civilian airplanes and landed them at a Jordanian airport. With 425 British and American lives at stake, the Palestinians seized international attention by appearing before American television cameras and stating their demands. The entire world learned how powerless the king had become. The commandos negotiated on their own. They refused to acknowledge or meet with Jordanian officials. It was as if Jordan had been replaced by a Palestinian state. The king and his laws did not exist. Hussein felt helpless and humiliated.

The hostages were eventually released unharmed, but the heinous act was the final step toward civil war. The army prepared to move with or without the king's permission. At one point, Hussein personally asked an army unit not to attack a PLO stronghold. "Discipline is required," the king told his men. "The time to fight is nearing," he said.

Hussein spoke the truth. On September 16, 1970, Amman radio crackled with an urgent message from the king, "A situation of uncertainty, chaos, and insecurity prevails in our dear country, and the danger which threatens Jordan has increased. We find it our duty to take a series of measures to restore

> *Jordan is ours, Palestine is ours, and we shall build our national entity on the whole of the land after having freed it of both the Zionist presence and the reactionary-traitor [Hussein] presence.*
> —YASIR ARAFAT
> leader of the Palestine
> Liberation Organization

law and order, and to preserve the life of every citizen, his means of living and his property," Hussein said. The statement meant war.

The next day, Hussein ordered a massive military offensive against Palestinian bases in Amman. The Jordanian army, which had been reequipped with British and American weapons, rolled tanks and armored personnel carriers toward the capital city. The fighting soon turned brutal as government troops met heavy resistance. The Palestinians fired mortars from rooftop bunkers. Government tanks responded with thunderous blasts. The battle raged from house to house, street to street. Civilians caught in the violence huddled in basements.

Before the battle began, Hussein planned to wipe out Palestinian resistance in less than 48 hours. This was a critical time period. After 48 hours, Hussein believed other Arab countries would come to the Palestinians' rescue. His only hope for success depended on speed. But the Palestinians were well trained in urban warfare. They continued fighting past the two-day deadline.

As expected, other Arab countries learned of the violence. Syria, which was extremely devoted to the Palestinians' cause, protested the most loudly. The Syrians had heard exaggerated reports about massacres of Palestinians. In response, they advanced their army to Jordan's northern border, and on September 20, 1970, the Syrians invaded Jordan.

Hussein's confidence collapsed. His troops were still bogged down in the streets of Amman. Under the circumstances, Jordan had little chance of defeating Syria's heavily equipped army. Women and children were evacuated. All troops were ordered to fight to the last man.

Outside the Middle East, Jordan's predicament attracted great concern. The country was friendly with both Britain and the United States. Syria was closely aligned with the Soviet Union. As has often been the case in Middle Eastern history, seemingly isolated outbursts carried broader dangers. In defense of Jordan, the United States moved troops into the region. The Soviet Union countered by increasing its naval fleet in the Mediterranean Sea. Battle

A group of Al-Fatah Palestinian guerrillas stand at attention at a ceremony attended by leader Yasir Arafat. Al-Fatah, one of the main groups within the PLO, was supported with money from Syria, but its raids against Israel were launched from Jordan.

A Red Cross convoy brings food into Amman in October 1970 after the city was ravaged by the bitter civil war between King Hussein's government troops and rebellious Palestinian guerrillas.

lines were drawn. A larger, international conflict seemed likely.

But a curious event then occurred. In late September, after some bitter fighting on the northern frontier, Syria inexplicably withdrew its army from Jordan. The retreat was sudden and unannounced. All invading troops and equipment were pulled back to Syria. Unknown to Hussein, the Soviet Union had secretly pressured Syria to retreat. The Soviets knew the war held potentially cataclysmic consequences. Further Syrian involvement would lead to retaliation by Jordan's allies. The Soviets persuaded the Syrians to withdraw, averting a major altercation between the superpowers. Hussein had survived once more.

Freed from Syria's threat, Hussein soon rid Amman of the Palestinian menace. He then turned his attention to defeating the PLO in other parts of his country. In the next year, Jordan's army waged a cruel and bloody campaign aimed at destroying all resistance. Strengthened by British and American military and financial support, Hussein's forces annihilated the Palestinian army. PLO bases were destroyed and rebel soldiers were hanged. Those commandos who survived the purge fled to Syria and Lebanon. In desperation, some crossed the Jordan River and hid in Israel. "I'd rather die on enemy

A British jetliner dissolves into debris and smoke as the Palestinian guerrillas who hijacked the plane to Jordan touch off explosives in September 1970. The hostages from three planes were released, but the incident was the catalyst for civil war in Jordan that fall.

A woman picks her way through the ruins of a building on the outskirts of Amman in October 1970. Hussein began an offensive against the PLO bases in Amman, and his army fought civilians as well as the PLO commandos, destroying large sections of Amman and other important cities.

soil than at the hands of an Arab brother," one commando told a newspaper reporter at the time. By August 1971 Hussein had gained a complete victory. There were no more PLO commandos operating in Jordan.

Throughout the bloodshed, other Arab countries stayed clear of the fighting. They voiced opposition to the Jordanian campaign against the Palestinians but refused to aid the commandos militarily. Egypt was particularly quiet. Nasser had died in 1970. His successor, Anwar Sadat, was too involved with Egyptian problems to worry about foreign concerns. With his neighbors silent, Hussein's goal was accomplished. His troops had eliminated the opposition without the rebels inciting foreign support. It was a great victory.

Yet the battle carried a heavy personal burden. Hussein now looked much older than his 35 years. His hair was thinning and gray at the temples. He appeared slightly stoop-shouldered, and his lively walk slowed in pace. He saw little of his family. His wife and children stayed in Britain during the most desperate hours of the civil war. Hussein and Muna were rarely seen together. Rumors of marital problems circulated among the couple's personal staff. The difficult years had not been good to Hussein.

King Hussein (foreground, second from left) dances with Bedouin troops in 1971. Strengthened by British and American military and financial support, Hussein's forces finally drove the PLO commandos from Jordan by August 1971.

8

The Road to Peace

The early 1970s was a time of realization for Hussein. Faced with the Arab defeat of 1967 and the ensuing civil war in his own country, the king now knew that Jordan's only course for survival was peaceful coexistence with Israel. The Israelis were courageous and skilled soldiers. The Arabs could not push them into the sea. Hussein realized that the future depended not on guns but negotiations. With this in mind, he met with Israeli officials and worked toward peacefully ending their occupation of the West Bank. "The Jordanians are more deeply involved with the problem than any other country or people, and we have to make our contribution toward a just and durable peace," Hussein told reporters in 1971.

Realizations were also occurring in Hussein's private life. Early in 1973 the king abruptly announced his divorce from Muna. He then married 24-year-old Alia Toukan, a beautiful, highly educated Jordanian Palestinian who worked for the country's national airline. Sources close to the king termed the marriage an affair of the heart. But critics condemned Hussein. Muna was a dutiful mother and wife who had won the admiration of many Jordanians. Hussein's callous disregard for her was viewed as typical Arab male chauvinism. "Arab men are obsessed by youth and beauty. When a loving

> *Almost unceasingly, enemies sought to destroy our small country; small, yet vital because of its strategic position, not only geographically but because of our unswerving, uncompromising stand for freedom and against communism, and our struggles to serve the principles and objectives of the Arab peoples.*
> —HUSSEIN

A portrait taken of King Hussein in 1971 on the occasion of Al-Fiter, the Muslim feast marking the end of the holy month of Ramadan. After Jordan's 1967 defeat by Israel and the civil war of 1970–71, Hussein began to search for a way to coexist peacefully with the state of Israel.

Israeli relatives of those who died in the October 1973 Yom Kippur War clutch the stones of the Western Wall in Jerusalem at the end of a day of fasting and meditation. The 19-day war, in which Egypt and Syria simultaneously attacked Israel on the Jewish holy day of Yom Kippur, saw some of the bloodiest fighting since the battles of World War II.

woman has lost one of these graces, she might as well hang up her veil and go home," wrote a reporter at the time. Muna did just that. After the separation, she and her four children returned to Britain to live with her parents. Hussein began a new life and later had a son and daughter by Alia.

Inside Jordan's government, Hussein's marriage to a Palestinian was seen as a wise political decision. The king needed Palestinian support for the peace plan he had developed. The plan called for a union between Jordan and the West Bank, and it established Hussein as the new region's ruler. The Israelis showed interest in the plan, believing Hussein's

moderate leadership would have a calming effect on the region. But West Bank Palestinians were less agreeable. They wanted their own independent country, free from Israel and Jordan. Even Hussein's new wife could not convince the Palestinians otherwise.

Other Arabs were even more opposed to the plan. Syria and Egypt argued that the only solution to Israeli occupation of Arab lands was war. So, on October 6, 1973, the Jewish holy Day of Atonement, the two nations launched a massive simultaneous military offensive against Israel — the Yom Kippur War. The conflict lasted only 19 days but contained some of the bloodiest and most intensive warfare since World War II. Although Syria and Egypt failed to expel Israel from Arab lands, their armies fought hard and inflicted substantial casualties.

Hussein refused to join the Arabs in the war. From the outset, he knew Israel would win the conflict. He also still hoped to resolve the problem through a peaceful federation between Jordan and the West Bank. Toward this end, the king negotiated with the Israelis, flying his own helicopter to prearranged meeting places. The talks failed, however, and Hussein's dream of regaining the West Bank was further shattered the following year at an Arab summit conference.

In October 1974, Arab leaders from throughout the Middle East met in the country of Morocco to declare the Palestine Liberation Organization the "sole legitimate representative of the Palestinian people." The action stripped Hussein of the right to negotiate with Israel concerning the West Bank. The king was relegated to a bystander in the peacemaking process. It was an embarrassing experience for Hussein. Jordan held legal title to the West Bank. Negotiations for its liberation should have been carried out by the king. His Arab brothers, however, were repaying a bitter debt. Jordan's neighbors had not forgotten Hussein's war against the Palestinian army in 1970 and his refusal to join in the Yom Kippur War of 1973. Their recognition of the PLO as peace representatives significantly decreased Hussein's influence in the Middle East.

> *Jordan today is an avowed and active member of the comity of free nations, despite the fact that it faces a complex pattern of hostilities. On one side we have Israel, which Jordan as much as any other Arab nation regards as a hostile force unjustly created in our midst, and helped by some nations of the world on many occasions since. On the other side are our sister Arab states, comrades against the common foe of Israel, but also frequently hostile to us.*
> —HUSSEIN

> *A nation's spirit and ability to survive are not determined by its size or population but by the will of its people, their faith in their country, their causes, and their determination to make their lives worthwhile.*
>
> —HUSSEIN

Israel quickly refused to negotiate with the PLO. The Israelis saw the PLO as an outlaw organization whose goal was the violent elimination of Israel. Since the war of 1973, PLO commandos had made Israel a daily target for terrorist attacks. The PLO bombed Israeli airports and threw hand grenades into the crowded streets of Jerusalem. The victims were often women and children. Peace between these bitter enemies was impossible. A more moderate representative was needed to voice Arab concerns. Hussein again seemed the logical choice. But personal tragedy stood in the way.

In February 1977 Hussein received a grim message. His wife, Alia, had been a passenger in a helicopter that crashed earlier in the day. The craft fell in a fiery ball on the rocky hills of Jordan. No survivors were found. "My precious companion has been lost," Hussein tearfully told his country later that night. The queen's death was a crushing event for the king. Hussein had respected Alia's intelligence and compassion, and he had loved her deeply. The king had fully expected to spend the rest of his life with her. But fate ran a different, cruel course.

As was his nature, Hussein grieved but soon overcame the tragedy. He was experienced in handling despair. It wasn't long before his life returned to normal. Then, in the winter of 1978, the king met another beautiful young woman. Lisa Halaby was unlike any woman Hussein had known before. She was tall, willowy, and an American. Educated at Princeton University, in the United States, she enjoyed art and athletics. She and the king soon discovered mutual interests in sailing, skiing, and driving fast cars. Their courtship lasted only two months before they were married on July 15, 1978. The announcement came so quickly that palace officials had little time to prepare for the ceremony. The seven-layer English wedding cake was still being iced an hour before the wedding. There was also little of the revelry that had surrounded the king's previous marriages.

The ceremony was kept small and simple. Lisa converted to Islam and took the name Noor al-Hus-

Two guerrillas who attacked an Israeli bus, killing more than 30 people. After the war of 1973, PLO commandos made Israel a daily target for terrorist attacks, often killing innocent people. Israel refused to negotiate with the PLO, the appointed representative of the Palestinians, thus ensuring that peace negotiations over the West Bank would include Jordan.

King Hussein with his fiancée, Lisa Halaby, in May 1978. Halaby, an American who converted to Islam and took the name Noor al-Hussein, or "Light of Hussein," became the king's fourth wife on July 15, 1978.

sein, or "Light of Hussein." The couple has since lived a happy life.

But while the king tended to his personal life, political events in the Middle East advanced at a rapid pace. With Hussein preoccupied, an unlikely figure emerged as an Arab peacemaker. In September 1978 President Anwar Sadat of Egypt accepted an invitation to meet with Prime Minister Menachem Begin of Israel and negotiate for peace in the Middle East. U.S. President Jimmy Carter hosted the meeting, which was held at Camp David, a presidential retreat in Maryland. An agreement was reached that ended hostilities between the two Middle Eastern countries.

Hussein refused to take part in the Camp David conference. The king believed that the Arab agreement of 1974 still recognized the PLO as the sole

President Anwar Sadat of Egypt, U.S. President Jimmy Carter, and Prime Minister Menachem Begin of Israel stand at attention during the playing of their national anthems at the peace negotiations between Egypt and Israel at Camp David, Maryland, in 1978. King Hussein refused to join the negotiations, feeling that Israel was not making great enough concessions to the Arabs.

Palestinian representative. Hussein also believed that Israel was using the conference to gain world support without making real concessions to the Arabs. "It seems that the parties have agreed only to disagree," Hussein commented in 1978.

Hussein's refusal to join the talks won great support in other Arab nations. Iraq, Syria, and Saudi Arabia agreed with Hussein's position and praised his courageous stand. Relations between Jordan and its neighbors improved dramatically during this period of good feeling. Iraq and Saudi Arabia loaned Hussein large sums of money, which he used to strengthen Jordan's troubled economy. As a result, the early 1980s brought unprecedented prosperity to Jordan. The number of jobs increased significantly. Jordanians found work making cement and mining phosphorus. Although still poor by American standards, the nation's economy grew at a healthy rate of 10 percent a year. People bought luxury items, such as radios, motorcycles, and imported clothing. Meat, milk, and cheese were available at small grocery stores. Men pooled their money and started small businesses and farms. More than half of the population now lived in cities. Even the Bedouins had ended their wandering and settled down to productive jobs in cities.

It was during this time of domestic stability that Hussein launched a new peace initiative. In March 1985 the king unveiled a proposal to have Israel meet directly with Jordanian and Palestinian representatives. The proposal included recognition of Israel's right to exist, a major step toward peace. In November 1985 Hussein traveled to Washington, D.C., to enlist support for his idea from U.S. President Ronald Reagan.

At the White House, Hussein expressed the need for urgent action. "We are offering a unique opportunity for peace which may not be with us for long," the king said. As he spoke, one could not help but admire the king's tenacity. In a region where power changes hands quickly, Hussein had persevered for 32 years, longer than any other Middle Eastern leader. He had faced many dangerous situations, yet emerged from each with his pride and power

A Palestinian commando drill exercise in Zalka, Jordan, during a visit of PLO Chairman Yasir Arafat in 1984. By this time, Hussein had allowed the PLO to reestablish some facilities within Jordan. Hussein's refusal to join the Camp David talks stemmed from his adherence to a 1974 Arab agreement that the PLO was the sole legal representative of the Palestinian people.

PLO leader Yasir Arafat (second from left) meets with Ayatollah Ruhollah Khomeini (left) of Iran in 1979. Khomeini's fundamentalist Islamic regime introduced another destabilizing factor into the volatile Middle East.

intact. Hussein believed his survival was God's will. Critics were less obliging. "He has survived only by the constant reassertion of his authority through the military," wrote Peter Snow in his 1971 biography of Hussein.

Yet Hussein was only a 17-year-old boy when he assumed the throne in 1953. At that time his grandfather was dead and his father was an invalid. Hussein had no role model to follow and, consequently, learned to lead through trial and error. Moreover, the boy inherited a poor and divided country. It was more the figment of a British mapmaker's imagination than a unified and independent nation. From this, the king built a national identity. Today the country's diverse people are Jordanians first and Bedouins, Arabs, and Palestinians second. The costs were great. Jordan lost many lives and much land during its difficult growing period. Whether the price was too high remains to be decided. But seeing Hussein before the podium that November day made one believe that an ultimate good would result from the king's reign. This man who came of age in violent times was now embarking on his most difficult assignment — preventing war. Hussein had witnessed much hatred and bloodshed. He had seen the full range of human motivation — hatred and love, fear and courage, loneliness and joy. Now Hussein looked for peace.

King Hussein (right), with Zeid Rifal, prime minister and minister of defense of Jordan, attends the United Nations General Assembly in New York in September 1985. Celebrating the 40th anniversary of the UN, Hussein traveled to the United States to gain support for his new peace initiative, which included recognition of Israel's right to exist.

UNITED NATIONS

Further Reading

Glubb, John. *A Soldier with the Arabs.* New York: Harper and Brothers, 1957.

Harris, George Lawrence. *Jordan.* New Haven, Connecticut: HRAF Press, 1958.

Hussein ibn Talal. *My War with Israel* (As told to and with additional material by Vick Vance and Pierre Lauer). New York: William Morrow and Co., Inc., 1969.

———. *Uneasy Lies the Head.* New York: Bernard Geis Associates, 1962.

Kimche, Jon. *The Second Arab Awakening.* New York: Holt, Rinehart and Winston, 1970.

Morris, James. *The Hashemite Kings.* New York: Pantheon Books, Inc., 1959.

Phillips, David and Peter Snow. *The Arab Hijack War: The True Story of September 1970.* New York: Ballantine Books, Inc., 1971.

Sinai, Anne and Allen Pollack, eds. *The Hashemite Kingdom of Jordan and The West Bank.* New York: American Academic Association for Peace in the Middle East, 1977.

Snow, Peter. *Hussein: A Biography.* London: Barrie and Jenkins, Ltd., 1972.

Trevelyan, Humphrey. *The Middle East in Revolution.* Boston, Massachusetts: Gambit, Inc., 1970.

Chronology

Nov. 14, 1935	Born Ibn Talal Hussein, grandson of Abdullah, first king of Jordan
May 1946	Jordan declares itself independent from Britain
May 14, 1948	Israel declares independence
1949	Hussein attends Victoria College, a boarding school in Alexandria, Egypt
July 20, 1951	Abdullah is assassinated in Jerusalem
July 23, 1951	Hussein's uncle, Naif, becomes ruler of Jordan
Sept. 1951	Hussein enrolls at Harrow, a preparatory school in Britain
Sept. 6, 1951	Hussein's father, Talal, replaces Naif as king of Jordan
Aug. 12, 1952	Talal is deposed by Jordan's Parliament; Hussein is declared king of Jordan
1952–53	Hussein attends Sandhurst Royal Military Academy in Britain
May 2, 1953	Officially inaugurated as king
Autumn 1955	Palestinians living in Jordan riot against the Baghdad Pact
March 1, 1956	Hussein dismisses British General Glubb as chief of staff of Jordan's army
1957	Thwarts attempted coup led by Army Chief of Staff Ali Abu Nuwar and calms Zerqa riots
Feb. 1, 1958	Egypt and Syria join to form the United Arab Republic
Feb. 14, 1958	Jordan and Iraq form the Arab Union
July 14, 1958	King Faisal II of Iraq is assassinated; soon afterward, Iraq joins the Arab anti-Hussein movement
Summer 1958	Jordan overcomes Arab boycott with U.S. and British aid
Jan. 1964	Arab leaders meeting in Egypt officially recognize the Palestine Liberation Organization (PLO) as responsible for Palestinian resistance to Israel
May 16, 1967	Egyptian President Gamal Abdel Nasser orders United Nations peacekeeping forces out of the Sinai peninsula
June 7, 1967	Israel attacks Egypt, commencing the Six-Day War
Sept. 16, 1970	Hussein declares war against PLO commandos in Jordan
Sept. 20, 1970	Syria invades Jordan in defense of the PLO, only to withdraw a few days later on orders from the U.S.S.R.
1971	Hussein rids Jordan of PLO commandos
Oct. 6, 1973	Yom Kippur War erupts between Israel and the combined forces of Egypt and Syria; Jordan remains neutral
Oct. 1974	The PLO is declared, at an Arab summit meeting in Morocco, to be the sole legitimate representative of the Palestinian people
Sept. 1978	Hussein refuses to take part in the U.S.-sponsored Egypt-Israel peace accord at Camp David
1985	Launches new peace initiative

Index

Abdullah ibn Hussein, king of Jordan
(grandfather), 15, 16, 17, 18, 21,
22, 25, 27, 28, 30–31, 32, 33, 34,
39, 61
Africa, 14
Alexandria, 27
al-Hussein, Muna (second wife), 74, 95, 97,
98
al-Hussein, Noor (fourth wife), 100
Amman, 14, 24, 25, 33, 43, 47, 49, 50, 57,
65, 67, 68, 76, 85, 88, 90, 93
Aqaba, 18
Arab nationalism, 28, 55, 56, 66, 70
Arab Solidarity Agreement, 65
Arab Union, 68
Ashu, Shukri, 34
Baghdad, 70
Baghdad Pact, 53, 57, 59, 61
Balfour Declaration, 21
Bedouins, 14, 16, 17, 18, 30, 44, 66, 67,
107
Begin, Menachem, 103
Bethlehem, 13, 85
Cairo, 17
Camp David conference, 103
Carter, Jimmy, 103
Churchill, Winston, 18
Eastern Roman Empire, 14
Egypt, 13, 17, 22, 27, 39, 51, 53, 55, 64,
65, 70, 75, 76, 78, 80, 94, 99, 103
Faisal I, king of Iraq (great-uncle), 18, 21,
41
Faisal II, king of Iraq (cousin), 41, 42, 43,
49–50, 55, 56, 68, 70, 75
Farouk, king of Egypt, 55
fedayeen, 86
France, 18, 65
Gardiner, Toni see al-Hussein, Muna
Germany, 17
Glubb, John Bagot, 28, 29, 52, 58, 61, 62,
63
Golan Heights, 82
Great Britain, 17, 18, 21, 22, 28, 42, 53,
55, 56, 57, 62, 65, 71, 90
Halaby, Lisa see al-Hussein, Noor
Hamed, Dina Abdul (first wife), 51
Harrow, 41, 70
Hashemite dynasty, 17, 18, 22, 41, 50

Hejaz, 17
Hussein ibn Ali (great-grandfather), 17, 18
Hussein ibn Talal, king of Jordan
Arab boycott and, 70, 71
Arab Union and, 68
assassination attempts on, 73–74,
88–89
birth, 14–15
Camp David accord and, 103–104
early years, 24–25
education, 25, 27, 28, 41, 42, 44, 45
King Abdullah and, 25, 27, 30–33
king of Jordan, 42, 45, 47, 49, 50, 62,
63, 74, 97, 98, 99
marriage, 51, 74, 97, 100
Nasser and, 58, 61
Palestine Liberation Organization and,
76, 85–86, 89–90, 93
peace talks proposal, 104
Six-Day War and, 13, 14, 81, 82–83, 85
Zerqa riots and, 67–68
Iraq, 13, 18, 21, 42, 49, 55, 56, 68, 70, 104
Islam, 14, 17
Israel, 13, 18, 21, 28, 29, 30, 45, 52, 53, 64,
65, 71, 76, 78, 80, 81, 82, 87, 88, 94,
97, 99, 100, 103, 104
Jericho, 13, 85
Jerusalem, 14, 18, 27, 31, 32, 33, 39, 85,
100
Jordan River, 13, 21, 29, 85, 94
Kitchener, Horatio, 17
Lawrence, T. E. ("Lawrence of Arabia"), 15,
16
Lebanon, 14, 18, 93
London, 28, 46
mansef, 43
Maryland, 103
Mecca, 14, 17, 18
Medina, 18
Mediterranean Sea, 65, 90
Middle East, 14, 17, 18, 21, 27, 28, 42, 55,
59, 62, 68, 75, 90, 103
Morocco, 99
Muhammad, 17
Nabulsi, Suleiman, 64, 65
Naif ibn Abdullah (uncle), 25, 40–41
Nasser, Gamal Abdel, 53–55, 56, 57, 58, 59,
61, 65, 68, 78, 80, 81, 94

New York Times, The, 65
Nuwar, Ali Abu, 63, 64, 65, 66, 67, 68
Ottoman Empire, 17, 18
Palestine *see* Israel
Palestine Liberation Organization (PLO), 75–76, 86, 87, 88, 89, 93, 94, 99, 100, 103
Palestinians, 29–30, 31, 52, 53, 55, 58, 59, 61, 66, 74, 80, 82, 85, 86, 89, 90, 99, 104, 107
Persian Gulf, 22
Princeton University, 100
Reagan, Ronald, 104
Red Sea, 18, 65
Sadat, Anwar, 94, 103
Samu, 76
Sandhurst Royal Military Academy, 44, 45, 46
Saudi Arabia, 14, 65, 68, 70, 75, 104
Sinai peninsula, 78, 82
Sinai War, 64–65
Six-Day War, 13, 14, 81, 82, 83
Snow, Peter, 106
Soviet Union, 55, 65, 90, 93

Suez Canal, 65
Switzerland, 42
Sykes-Picot Agreement, 18
Syria, 13, 14, 18, 21, 65, 68, 70, 75, 78, 90, 93, 94, 99, 104
Talal ibn Abdullah, king of Jordan (father), 15, 25, 39, 40, 41, 42
Toukan, Alia (third wife), 97, 98, 100
Transjordan, 14, 18
Turkey, 55
United Arab Republic (U.A.R.), 68, 70
United Nations, 28, 65, 78
United States, 32, 66, 71, 90, 100
University of Jordan, 74
Victoria College, 27, 28, 33, 41
Washington, D.C., 104
West Bank, 13, 29, 66, 76, 82, 85, 97, 98, 99
World War I, 15, 17
World War II, 28
Yom Kippur War, 99
Zain, queen of Jordan (mother), 15, 42, 50
Zerqa, 67

Gregory Matusky graduated with honors from the University of Pennsylvania. He holds degrees in communications, English, and marketing, and he has worked in public relations and business consulting.

John P. Hayes, Ph.D., is a Philadelphia freelance writer and college professor. He is the author of *James A. Michener: A Biography* and several other books and many articles. Dr. Hayes, his wife, and three children reside in North Hills, Pennsylvania.

Arthur M. Schlesinger, jr., taught history at Harvard for many years and is currently Albert Schweitzer Professor of the Humanities at City University of New York. He is the author of numerous highly praised works in American history and has twice been awarded the Pulitzer Prize. He served in the White House as special assistant to Presidents Kennedy and Johnson.